O R I G I N A L
C H E V R O L E T
C A M A R O
1 9 6 7 - 1 9 6 9

ORIGINAL CHEVROLET CAMARO

1967-1969

The Restoration Guide

JASON SCOTT

PHOTOGRAPHY BY ANDY KRAUSHAAR

DEDICATION

For Cameron, the best little buddy a dad could hope for. *Jason*

Inspiring | Educating | Creating | Entertaining

Brimming with creative inspiration, how-to projects, and useful information to enrich your everyday life, Quarto Knows is a favorite destination for those pursuing their interests and passions. Visit our site and dig deeper with our books into your area of interest: Quarto Creates, Quarto Cooks, Quarto Homes, Quarto Lives, Quarto Drives, Quarto Explores, Quarto Gifts, or Quarto Kids.

This edition published in 2019 by Motorbooks, an imprint of The Quarto Group,
100 Cummings Center, Suite 265D, Beverly, MA 01915 USA.
T (978) 282-9590 F (978) 283-2742
www.QuartoKnows.com

Motorbooks titles are also available at discount for retail, wholesale, promotional, and bulk purchase. For details, contact the Special Sales Manager by email at specialsales@quarto.com or by mail at The Quarto Group, Attn: Special Sales Manager, 100 Cummings Center, Suite 265D, Beverly, MA 01915 USA.

10 9 8 7 6 5 4 3 2 1

ISBN: 978-0-7603-6590-8

Acquiring Editor: Zack Miller
Design: Chris Fayers

Printed in China

Contents

Introduction

Although there have been four distinct "generations" of Camaros, the originals—the 1967 through 1969 models—are still considered most desirable by collectors and enthusiasts.

Few cars have so entrenched themselves in American history that they have made the leap to become a household word, recognized and appreciated by nearly everyone, regardless of age, race, color, or creed. Chevrolet's Camaro is just such a car.

From its introduction in the fall of 1966 right through today, the Camaro has continued to be at the top of the performance-car heap, year after year. That legacy—along with the Camaro's exciting, attractive styling—has helped make the Camaro a prized collector's item, as well as a popular street machine.

Time, however, has taken its toll on Camaros, whittling away the pool of available cars from which collectors can select. The reduction in numbers has had an inverse effect on Camaro values, causing prices for even base models in original condition to climb into five-digit ranges.

Whether you're a hard-core collector looking for a truly rare Camaro or an excited enthusiast, it pays to be aware of what makes one Camaro different from another, what makes one "rare" versus common, what makes one "correct" versus incorrect in terms of originality, and, ultimately, what makes one worth more money than another.

This book is intended to give you a good look at what *original* first-generation Camaros were like when they left the Norwood or Van Nuys assembly plants. We've attempted to locate excellent unrestored Camaros as well as painstakingly restored examples that illustrate how parts should look, what parts were included with what options, and otherwise to show all the subtle differences that make a typical "restored" Camaro easy to identify as restored versus original.

To back up the photography, we've compiled a wealth of data and information that describe and document the installed parts and their typical finishes, to serve as both reference material and refinishing guidebook.

We would like to thank all the collectors and restorers that provided help to us: Bill Brown, Milton Bullard, Dave Canedo, Larry Christianson, Jim Elliot, Rick Freeman, Rob Fridenberg, Wes Grand, Nick Haglund, Donald and Kim Hanville, Eric Hummel, Dee Hutsler, Dave Kalish, Patrick Lewis, Ken Lucas, Jim McGlynn, Bob Moore, Brent Roby, Jim Parks, Guy Price, Donald Smith, Todd Sullivan, and Don Viers. Thanks also to Jim Keliher of the Worldwide Camaro Association.

Creating this book was the pleasure of a lifetime and gave us a wonderful opportunity (excuse?) to seek out some of the finest Camaros in the country and to spend time with them and their owners. We hope you enjoy the book and find it as enjoyable and helpful as we found it fun.

Andy Kraushaar and
Jason Scott

Chapter 1
1967 Camaro

Identification

Because the Camaro was a new model for Chevrolet, identifying it was pretty easy at the time it appeared—there weren't any cars like it on the road. But as soon as the similar-looking 1968 models arrived (and later the 1969s), telling one model year from another became somewhat more complex. Fortunately, there are a number of identifiers on the vehicle, both those that are used for legal purposes, as well as a number of general styling traits and cues, that differentiate the cars.

Vehicle Identification Number (VIN)

The vehicle identification number (VIN, for short) is used to legally identify and differentiate one vehicle from any other on the road. Nineteen sixty-seven Camaros featured a small tin tag stamped with the manufacturer's name ("CHEVROLET") and the vehicle's unique VIN. The tags measure approximately ¾ inches tall by 3 inches long and were stamped from behind, producing raised characters and numbers. VIN tags were affixed to the forward driver's door hinge pillar post, utilizing two rivets with non-standard

This 1967 Rally Sport Camaro is a shiny example of how even a non-performance model benefits from the Camaro's race-inspired styling and on-track performances.

heads (to make recognizing tampered VINs easy), one through each end of the tag. Installation took place prior to painting of the body structure, so the tag itself and the rivets that secure it to the body should be painted body color. Unlike later Camaros, the 1967 Camaro VIN tags are not visible from outside the vehicle.

For information on how to decode Camaro VIN tags, please refer to Appendix A.

Trim Data Tag

The trim tag is another tin tag mounted to the upper left cowl (firewall) panel, inside the engine compartment, adjacent to the windshield wiper motor. The original purpose of the tag was to identify the specific vehicle's body style, original paint treatment, interior trim equipment, and specific accessories for service repair purposes. The tags also contain coded data to represent when the vehicle was built (the week of assembly) and the plant at which it was assembled.

For information on how to decode Camaro trim tags, please refer to Appendix B.

Engine Stamping

VIN and trim tags were not nearly as all-inclusive as modern vehicle information decals, which list not only the VIN and trim data, but also RPO (Regular Production Option) codes for options included on the vehicle.

One critical shortcoming of the old VIN and data tag systems was that neither precisely identified the exact engine that the vehicle was supposed to have installed underhood. General Motors (GM) partially overcame this shortcoming by stamping the engine model and partial VIN into a flat machined pad along the front of the engine.

The stamping consisted of two sets of characters. The first set utilized a two-letter code to identify the engine "model," plus the assembly date and plant information. The second set of characters was a partial VIN sequence that matched the engine assembly to the specific vehicle. Thus, the engine can be positively identified as a particular model (such as a Z28's 302), and positively linked to the vehicle, which helps to certify that a particular vehicle was equipped with a specific performance package (or not). The catch to engine stampings is that they are often machined off when an engine is rebuilt (specifically, when the cylinder case deck surfaces are milled), and false codes can be restamped.

General Recognition Info

Apart from the "official" identification each 1967 Camaro has—VIN, trim tag, engine stampings, and so on—there are a number of other ways to identify a 1967 model from a distance.

The first thing to determine is that a particular vehicle is, in fact, a first-generation (1967–1969) Camaro. Most enthusiasts will have little trouble doing this, though from a distance 1970–1971 Plymouth Barracudas and Dodge Challengers do bear more than a passing resemblance to Chevy's original pony car.

Of the three years that comprise the first-generation Camaro era, the 1969 models look considerably different due to all-new sheet metal that year (for more info on the specific characteristics of 1969 models, please refer to chapter 3, which covers them in detail). Discerning a 1967 model from a 1968 is less simple, because only fairly subtle differences exist between the two.

From the sides, you get two distinct clues. The first clue is that 1967 Camaros are the only Camaros to feature separate vent windows; later models use a single large piece of glass. Your second clue—and one that's particularly handy at night—is that 1967 Camaros are not equipped with side marker lamps on the front and rear fenders.

Spotting a 1967 Camaro from the front is a bit of a challenge, as well, unless you know what to look for. The easiest thing to look for are the turn signal lamps: non–Rally Sport 1967 models use round turn signal lamps mounted in the grille,

Nineteen sixty-seven was the only year that the Vehicle Identification Number (VIN) tag was affixed to the driver's side door hinge pillar, as shown here. The tag was installed (with two rivets) prior to the body structure being painted, thus it should be body color.

The long-hood/short-deck
body design (above) was
hardly new, yet Chevy
stylists worked wonders
with it for the Camaro.
With generous, rounded
wheelwells, fluid lines,
and gentle curves, the
first-year Camaro had a
sporty look that was
distinctly American
yet reminiscent of
European sports cars.
From the rear (right),
the Camaro's wide, low
taillamps mimicked the
car's overall appearance.
A gas cap–mounted
emblem identified the
model, plus you could spot
an RS model by the
presence of back-up lamps
below the bumper in the
valance panel.

inboard of the headlamps (1968s use rectangular turn signals). Nineteen sixty-seven Camaros equipped with the Rally Sport package (RPO Z22) had square marker turn signal lamps relocated to the lower valance panel—just like the 1968 models. The only difference is the grille, which for 1967 is composed of numerous small squares versus the rectangles used for 1968.

All first-generation Camaros have a similar appearance from the rear as well; however, there are subtle clues to help you distinguish a 1967 from a 1968 from a 1969. The most obvious differences all involve the tail lamp assemblies. Nineteen sixty-seven and 1968 assemblies are nearly identical, while 1969 units are much longer. Nineteen sixty-seven tail lamp bezels are a simple, rectangular-shaped chrome surround with the inside area of the bezel painted semigloss black. Nineteen sixty-eight units, although similar, have a vertical rib that divides each tail lamp into two halves.

If you happen to be run over by a first-generation Camaro and have the presence of mind to look at the rear shock absorber configuration, only the 1967 models have both shocks mounted to the forward side of the rear axle housing. Z28 and Super Sport (SS) models also featured a special torque rod to control rear axle windup and wheel hop under hard acceleration. The rod is attached to the right side of the rear axle assembly and to the chassis, beneath the right rear seat. (You can also spot these simply by looking underneath the car, either from the sides or the rear.)

It's worth noting that a number of items on 1967 Camaros are stamped or cast with part numbers and serial numbers. It is also possible to utilize these numbers to identify (or at least verify) that a 1967 Camaro is a 1967 model equipped with specific standard or optional equipment.

Body

The appearance of 1967 Camaro bodies is a large part of the reason for the models' popularity. The Camaro looked unlike anything else on the road; many buyers were attracted to its curvaceous sheet metal and liked its sporty appearance. Unlike some cars on the market, the Camaro utilized the same body panels for its top-performance models as for the base model, except for some hoods, so every Camaro was equally exciting, equally stylish.

Body Styles

The Camaro was available in two body styles: a semifastback two-door coupe, and a similar-looking two-door convertible. Sticking to just two body styles ensured that buyers of base models would be rewarded with a car every bit as attractive as any other Camaro model. For Chevrolet, it also meant a cost savings: the company only had to make two sets of body panels, unlike Ford, which had three Mustang body styles to contend with. Furthermore, Chevrolet designed the Camaro coupe and convertible models to share a maximum number of body panels, in effect cutting the panel designs to a single, cost-effective, and attractive design.

Hoods

Two basic Camaro hoods were available in 1967: a basic, flat steel hood with a subtle center crease running the length of the hood from front to rear; SS models were equipped with a similar hood that also featured a squarish raised section to which pot metal grille inserts were fitted for SS models. The inserts featured lengthwise fins, though some

1967 CAMARO PRODUCTION FIGURES

RPO	Description	Units
12337	Camaro sport coupe (6-cyl)	53,523
12367	Camaro convertible (6-cyl)	5,285
12437	Camaro sport coupe (V-8)	142,242
12467	Camaro convertible (V-8)	19,856
L35	Super Sport package w/325-hp 396-ci V-8	4,003
L48	Super Sport package w/295-hp 350-ci V-8	29,270
L78	Super Sport package w/375-hp 396-ci V-8	1,138
Z22	Rally Sport package	64,842
Z28	Special Performance package	602

1967 CAMARO COLOR AND TRIM COMBINATIONS

		INTERIOR TRIM COLORS AND RPO CODES							
		Gold 709	Blue 717	Black 760	Turq.	Red 741	Bright Blue	Parch./Black	Yellow
Models 12437/12467		709	717	760		741			
Deluxe Bucket Seat Option		711		765	779	742	732	797	707
Sport Cpe. Std. Int. Bench Seat		796	739	756					
Sport Cpe. Deluxe Int. Bench Seat		712		767		716			

EXTERIOR PAINT AND RPO CODES

RPO	Color	Stripe(s)	Gold	Blue	Black	Turq.	Red	Bright Blue	Parch./Black	Yellow
A A	Tuxedo Black	White	X	X	X	X	X	X	X	X
C C	Ermine White	Black	X	X	X	X	X	X	X	X
D D	Nantucket Blue	White			X	X		X	X	
E E	Deepwater Blue	White			X	X		X	X	
F F	Marina Blue	White*		X	X			X	X	
G G	Granada Gold	Black	X		X				X	X
H H	Mountain Green	Black			X				X	
K K	Emerald Turquoise	Black			X	X			X	
L L	Tahoe Turquoise	White			X	X			X	
M M	Royal Plum	White			X				X	
N N	Madiera Maroon	White	X		X		X		X	
R R	Bolero Red	White*			X		X		X	
S S	Sierra Fawn	Black	X		X				X	X
T T	Capri Cream	Black	X		X				X	X
Y Y	Butternut Yellow	Black			X	X	X		X	X

*Marina Blue and Bolero Red Camaros equipped with Black vinyl or convertible tops received Black stripes.
"Convertible tops were available in White, Black, or Medium Blue with any exterior color."
Vinyl tops were available in Black or Light Fawn with any exterior color.

The Camaro came in only two body styles: coupe or convertible, unlike Ford's Mustang, which had three. Lacking a fastback, both Camaros looked remarkably similar.

The base Camaro hood (right) in 1967 was largely flat and featureless, except for the center ridge and subtle depressions that lead back to the cowl panel vents. Underneath, a modest insulation blanket reduced noise from the engine. The only optional hood in 1967 was the SS-style hood, which actually came in two configurations, depending on the engine beneath it. Cars powered by a 350 received the SS hood with simulated hood vent grilles with full-length fins (below). The second SS-style hood (below right) was the same hood but had grilles that resembled four vent "stacks." This was installed on 396-powered Super Sport Camaros.

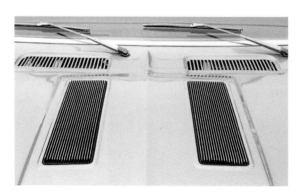

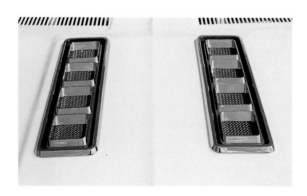

1967 SS-396 models have been seen with 1968 SS-396-style inserts with four simulated vent stacks per insert. Contrary to popular belief, 1967 Z28 models were not equipped with the "cowl induction" hood that became available in 1969 as the RPO ZL2 Special Ducted Hood, called the "Super Scoop" hood in Chevrolet advertisements.

Grille Assemblies

Two grille assemblies were used on 1967 Camaro models. Cars that were not equipped with RPO Z22 Rally Sport equipment received the standard grille assembly, which featured a black plastic grille comprised of horizontal and vertical slats that formed a gridwork. The grille had a subtle, forward-pointing "V" shape but was relatively shallow, compared to later Camaros. Tin headlight bezels surround each of the two single-unit headlamps. Two round directional signal lamp assemblies were mounted to the center grille section, which featured chromelike plating on the directional signal lamp surrounds.

Rally Sport (RS) models received a completely different grille assembly that featured electrically operated swing-away headlamp doors that concealed the headlamps when closed. RS turn signal lamps were relocated to the lower valance panel, and were square, not round as on non-RS models. Again, the grille was cast of black plastic with a gridwork pattern. Headlamp units were still round, but did not feature any bezels, just tin retaining rings. The headlamp doors are cast plastic secured to a metal frame, which in turn connects to the electric motors.

Front Bumper

All 1967 Camaros were equipped with the same front bumper design: a chromed, stamped-steel unit that wraps around each side of the car and extends a few inches alongside the front fender toward the wheel opening. The bumper is secured to four steel brackets by four smooth-headed, chromed bumper bolts.

Front bumper guards were available under RPO V31 and consisted of vertical, chromed steel housings, each with a black rubber rub strip on its forward surface.

Rear Bumper

Like the front bumper, there was only a single rear bumper design for 1967 Camaros. The rear bumper was a chromed steel assembly that wrapped around the sides of the car and was secured to four steel brackets by a single chromed bumper bolt at each bracket. RPO V32 added vertical bumper guards to the rear bumper, and like the front bumper guards, the units were chromed, stamped steel with rubber rub strips.

Sides

The sides of 1967 Camaros were made up of four primary sheet-metal panels: the front fender, the door panel, the rear fender ("quarter panel"), and the rocker panel, beneath the doors. Only the quarter panel design differed between coupe and convertible models; the other panels were interchangeable.

This close-up of a 1967 Super Sport clearly shows the standard (non-RS) front grille and headlamp treatment, the SS "bumblebee stripe," and the "SS" ornamentation.

Here, the Rally Sport headlamp doors and relocated turn signal indicator lamps result in a dramatically different look for the RS Camaro. Note that "SS" ornamentation takes precedence over "RS" emblems.

The 1967 door handle was made of chrome-plated pot metal, while the door lock cylinder was stainless steel for durability.

The fenders and quarter panels featured subtle flares that accentuated the wheel openings. In addition, a pronounced crease delineated the upper body from the lower.

Several options added bright trim moldings to the wheel openings, the rocker panel, and even the A-pillars, between the front windshield and the side window glass. RPO Z21 added bright trim to the wheel openings and roof drip rails (except convertibles). RPO Z22 added bright trim along the top of the rocker panel, the fender, and the quarter panel. RPO Z23 added bright trim to the A-pillars.

Paint accent stripes were also available under RPO Z21. For more on stripes, see "Stripes and Bodyside Moldings" later in chapter 6.

Note that 1967 Camaros do not feature side marker lamps.

1967 Camaros were the only Camaros to feature a vent window. Also note that the vinyl top covers the A-pillar, between the windshield and side window.

Roof

Nineteen sixty-seven Camaro roofs came in three varieties: painted steel, vinyl-covered steel, and convertible.

Since two-tone paint options were not available, painted steel roofs were always body color. Drip rails were body color unless a vinyl top was ordered. Vehicles not equipped with a vinyl top, but equipped with either RPO Z21 or Z22, were treated to bright drip rail moldings. Convertible models did not feature drip rails.

Vinyl roof covers were glued to a semifinished steel roof. The vinyl covers consisted of four to six individual pieces of vinyl material: a large center section that covered the bulk of the roof; one piece per side that covered the C-pillars and approximately the first 8 inches of the sides of the roof; a fourth piece was used below the rear window and stretched approximately halfway to the deck lid along the filler panel. Unless RPO Z23 was ordered, the A-pillar windshield posts were each covered by a sheet of vinyl. (RPO Z23 provided trim that covered the A-pillar posts.) Bright trim was used to secure the ends of the vinyl along the drip rail, along the bottom of the C-pillars, and across the deck lid filler panel. Vinyl roofs were available in black or off-white, to match or contrast with the vehicle's paint color.

Convertible tops were available in three colors: black, medium blue, and white. The top material was a canvas fabric with a sewn-in clear vinyl rear window. The top's framework was primarily steel, and was available in either manual or power-operated configurations. The forward edge of the roof was secured by two latches to an oversized windshield header trimmed in bright metal. Where the top met the body panels on the sides and rear of the car, bright metal trim secured the fabric to the body.

Glass/Windows

Nineteen sixty-seven Camaro windows were manufactured by Libby Owens Ford and are easily identifiable thanks to their "LOF" and "Safety Flo-Lite" etching marks. In addition, the windows feature date-coding that makes it possible to determine the originality of the window.

Tinted windows were available under RPO A01 (all windows) and A02 (windshield only). Electrically operated power side windows were available under RPO A31.

The windshield is laminated safety glass, which breaks on impact but does not shatter.

The side and rear windows are safety plate glass, which shatters on impact.

The windshield and rear window are secured to the vehicle with a ropelike bead of black adhesive. Bright metal trim attaches to anchors secured to the window channel and fills the gap between the glass and the window channel, covering the trim and minimizing the amount of debris that can enter the window channel and cause water drainage problems.

The side windows are moveable: the vent windows rotate open, the doors' side windows slide up and down vertically within channels, and quarter windows tilt downward along a channel concealed within the quarter panel.

A rear window defroster was available via RPO C50 and consisted of a blower motor that mounted to the underside of the rear package shelf and utilized a grille that mounted to the top of the shelf. When activated by the switch on the instrument panel, the motor circulated warm air from within the passenger compartment against the rear window.

Mirrors

All 1967 Camaros came with two mirrors: a rearview mirror mounted inside the vehicle, hung from a support connected to the windshield header; and a round outside rearview mirror, mounted toward the front of the driver's door on a chrome-plated pot metal stand. An outside rearview mirror was not available for the passenger's door.

The driver's outside rearview mirror was available in a remote-control version, which utilized a miniature joysticklike control lever and a complex assembly of cables to tilt and swivel the mirror. The remote-control system was available as RPO D33.

Headlamps

All 1967 Camaros utilized two large, round, sealed beam headlamp units; one lamp was mounted to each side of the grille. Original-equipment lamp units were supplied by Guide and are identifiable by a triangle shape cast into the center of the lens with "T-3" in its center.

Unless Rally Sport equipment (RPO Z22) was ordered, the headlamp units were exposed at all times, and were surrounded by a metal bezel.

When RPO Z22 was ordered, the headlamps were concealed (when not in use) behind electrically operated doors that rotated around the center axis of the headlamp unit, and stowed beside the headlamp, toward the center of the vehicle. The headlamp doors featured a metal framework with a black plastic cover that matched the grille design. When the headlamp doors were closed, hiding the headlamps, the 1967 Camaro front end presented a clean, menacing appearance. Unfortunately, the electrical headlamp door actuators proved to be expensive, complex, and unreliable. Chevrolet later redesigned the system for 1968 and replaced the electric motors with vacuum-operated actuators, which later also proved to be unreliable.

1967 CAMARO MONTHLY PRODUCTION

	1967 Models			
	Los Angeles		Norwood	
Month	Start	End	Start	End
August (08)	100001	100491	100001	104143
September (09)	100492	105047	104144	112705
October (10)	105048	113101	112706	126720
November (11)	113102	124382	126721	141482
December (12)	124383	131165	141483	165657
January (01)	131166	138982	165658	181082
February (02)	138983	144958	181083	185266
March (03)	144959	151250	185267	197870
April (04)	151251	155897	197871	213722
May (05)	155898	159500	213723	228760
June (06)	159501	163266	228761	251048
July (07)	163267	165008	251049	254698

Figures courtesy of the United States Camaro Club   (Note: Monthly start/end units are approximate)

The exterior rearview mirror was a round, chromed mirror with a small "bow tie" insignia on the back.

Taillamps

Two taillamp designs were used on 1967 Camaros, depending on whether or not Rally Sport equipment (RPO Z22) was ordered. In either case, the car had two taillamp assemblies—one per side. RS-equipped models also featured separate back-up lamps that were mounted below the rear bumper, in the rear valance panel.

The Rally Sport taillamps featured separate back-up lamps, mounted beneath the bumper in the valance panel, so the inner taillamps were all red, as seen here. Note that the chrome exhaust extension was not available from the factory.

The lamp assemblies were set into the metal taillamp panel and were each trimmed with a chromed pot metal bezel. The bezels were secured from within the trunk using sheet-metal nuts that screwed onto posts cast into the bezel.

Taillamp lenses are date-coded and have a code identifying their intended use.

The taillamp assemblies use only clear bulbs.

Turn Signals

As with taillamp assemblies, two front turn signal lamp designs were utilized in 1967. The first design was for non-RS models and featured round lamp assemblies mounted in the grille, inboard of the headlamps. The lamps used amber or yellow-colored bulbs and clear lenses.

Rally Sport models, on the other hand, used square turn signal assemblies recessed into the outboard ends of the lower front valance panel. The lamp assemblies featured clear lenses and amber or yellow bulbs.

Marker Lamps

Nineteen sixty-seven Camaros do not have side marker lamps.

Back-up Lamps

Back-up lamps were integral with the taillamp assemblies on non–Rally Sport Camaros in 1967. A rounded rectangle of translucent plastic was inset into the inboard section of each taillamp assembly. A clear bulb was used.

Rally Sport models featured separate back-up lamps mounted beneath the rear bumper, in the rear valance panel. An opaque plastic lens mounted inside a chrome-plated metal bezel added a stylish touch to the assemblies.

Fuel Filler Cap

The fuel filler neck is located in the center of the taillamp panel on all 1967 Camaros. The standard gas cap featured the tribar Camaro logo. Super Sport models were given a cap with "SS" initials on it. Rally Sport models were equipped with a cap with "RS" initials, unless also equipped with Super Sport equipment, in which case the "SS" cap was used. Z28 models used the standard Camaro cap, unless Rally Sport equipment was included, in which case the "RS" cap was used. Z28 models never were equipped with the "SS" cap, as the models were mutually exclusive.

Deck Lid

All 1967 Camaros utilized the same deck lid assembly, regardless of body style or options. The assembly is largely rectangular in shape, and rather flat and featureless. It featured two large hinges at its forward edge. A "Chevrolet Camaro" emblem was secured to the deck lid's right rear corner.

Taillamps are another way to quickly identify the year of a particular Camaro, not to mention whether it is equipped with the Rally Sport (RPO Z22) option. The standard 1967 taillamp assembly featured an integral backup lamp and an appearance of two lamps per side.

For non-RS cars, the taillamp lenses were red rounded rectangles, divided into two "halves" by chromelike paint that gave the appearance of two lamp units per lens. The outboard section was fully red, while the inboard section featured a white rounded rectangle inset into it to serve as the backup lamp.

Rally Sport models used lenses that were solid red, since the back-up lamps were separate assemblies. Bezels were also painted semigloss black on RS models, except for the outer edge, which remained chrome plated.

In either case, the taillamp assemblies served as taillamps, brake lamps, and turn signals. Non-RS models also provided backup lamp functions.

If you didn't notice the RS-specific taillamps, the emblem on the gas cap should have caught your attention (below left). The SS-350 emblem was also easily identifiable on the gas cap (below right).

Here you can see the shape and contour of the optional rear spoiler, which was not widely available in 1967.

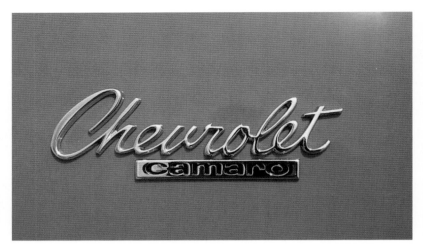

Stripes and Bodyside Moldings

A number of different striping treatments were applied to 1967 Camaros, from simple pinstriping along the sides to the broad, bold stripes applied to the hood and deck lid of Z28s.

Pinstripes were applied to the sides of 1967 Camaros ordered with RPO Z21 Style Trim Group or RPO Z22 Rally Sport equipment. A dual stripe began near the top of the front fender and followed the length of the fender, along the top of the door, and then along the top of the quarter panel.

Front Accent Band was Chevrolet's name for the "bumblebee stripe" that wrapped around the front of the car, starting at or slightly above the bumper line on each fender, ran up the fender (breaking temporarily for any model identification emblems, usually "RS" or "SS"), and continued onto the front header panel, just forward of the hood. The stripe band was actually three stripes: a broad solid band in between two thin pinstripes. Front accent bands were originally only applied as part of the Super Sport packages (RPOs L48, L35, or L78); however, a front accent band was made available later in the year for any Camaro under RPO D91.

The deck lid emblem (above) was the same as the front header panel emblem: "Chevrolet Camaro". The dual hood and deck lid stripes of the Z/28 (below) were commonly added by owners to non-Z Camaros. Though the stripes were not available on convertibles in 1967 (since RPO Z28 required a coupe), this convertible's stripe application is largely correct in appearance, starting on the deck lid filler panel. Note that factory-applied stripes did not have paint beneath the deck lid emblems, thanks to a small template used by painters on the assembly line.

Deck Lid Spoiler

Contrary to popular belief, a deck lid spoiler was not offered from the factory on 1967 Camaros. Spoilers were, however, available for dealer installation and were fairly popular. The spoiler, made of fiberglass, required that holes be drilled through the deck lid for the spoiler's mounting studs to protrude through. Sheet-metal "speed" nuts were used to secure the spoiler to the deck lid.

On vehicles that were equipped with RPO Z28 and the dealer-installed spoiler, the spoiler was applied over the deck lid stripes, which were applied at the factory. (Later, factory-installed spoilers were installed prior to application of the stripes, so the area beneath the spoiler did not have striping paint.)

The base Camaro emblem, as seen in this 1967 grille, consisted of the Chevy "bow tie" logo on a striped background. A similar emblem was mounted on the gas cap in the rear of the car.

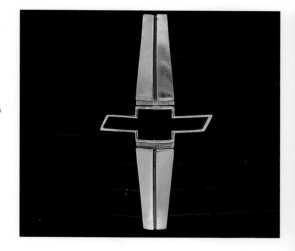

When RPO Z22 Rally Sport equipment was ordered, the base emblems were replaced by these "RS" emblems (far right) on the grille and gas cap, among other RS equipment changes.

On cars eqipped with wrap-around nose stripes, the header panel emblem was set atop the stripe, using it as the background.

"Z28" Stripes were referred to as "special paint stripes" under RPO Z28's description and were said to be applied to the hood and rear deck. In truth, the two broad (14.7-inch) stripes started on the front header panel (forward of the hood), ran back along the hood, onto the cowl panel between the hood and the windshield, skipped the roof, then resumed on the rear deck filler panel, and along the deck lid itself. The stripes were each trimmed by a pinstripe that started on one side, wrapped around the end of the stripe, and then continued down the other side of the main stripe. At the factory, special "masks" were used to prevent paint from being applied where emblems were secured on the deck lid. While the stripes were a part of RPO Z28, they could be "deleted" by simply noting so on the order sheet.

Window Moldings consisted of bright metal trim surrounding the windshield and rear window of all 1967 Camaros.

Lower Bodyside Moldings were included with RPO Z22 Rally Sport equipment. The bright metal trim attached along a body accent crease just above the rocker panel. Three pieces were used per side: one on the rear portion of each front fender, a second piece along each door, and the third on the front portion of the rear quarter panel.

Wheel Opening Moldings were installed on cars ordered with RPO Z21 or RPO Z22. The moldings were bright metal.

Roof Drip Rail Moldings were also part of options RPO Z21 (Style Trim Group), RPO Z22 (Rally Sport equipment), and RPO Z23 (Special Interior Group). These bright metal moldings could be installed on any coupe, but were not installed on convertible models.

Vinyl Roof Moldings were installed to secure the edges of the vinyl material. Bright metal moldings were secured to the base of the A-pillar, along the roof drip rail, along the base of the C-pillar, and along the deck lid filler panel. Windshield and rear window trim was used to secure the fabric in those areas.

Door Edge Guards, RPO B93, were a popular and inexpensive way to protect the rear edge of the doors from scratches and paint chips that could result from the occasional bump against another car or a wall.

Vinyl Bodyside Molding was available as a dealer-installed option and was quite popular. Available in several colors to match or contrast with the car's paint color, the adhesive-backed trim was applied to the midbody crease along the side of the vehicle, on the rear of the front fender, the door, and the front of the rear quarter panel.

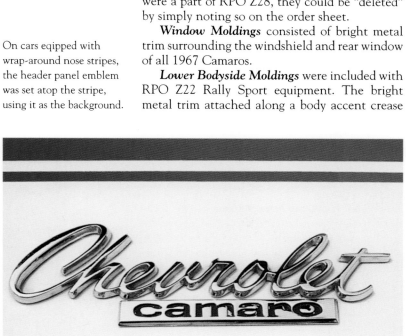

Two styles of "SS" emblems were available. The first style (far left), "SS-350", was installed on SS models equipped with the L48 350. The second style (left), simply the letters "SS", was used on 396-powered SS models in 1967.

In addition to grille emblems, 1967 Camaros frequently featured model identification emblems on the forward edge of the fenders, as this RS model (far left) shows. Similarly, SS models (left) sported identification on their fenders.

The engine designation was presented beneath the "Camaro" emblem on the rear of the front fenders, in 1967, as this emblem (far left) for a 350 V-8 shows. The "396 TurboJet" emblem (left) was similar, yet different enough that eagle-eyed challengers had fair warning before being outrun.

Emblems and Graphics

A variety of different emblems and graphic decals were used on 1967 Camaro models, depending upon the model and options ordered.

Header Panel and Deck Lid Emblems consisted of two pieces, each chrome-plated plastic. Because the Camaro was a new model and Chevrolet wanted to ensure buyers were aware it was a Chevy, the larger of the two emblems was a cursive script "Chevrolet". Beneath that, a rectangular bar had the word "camaro" recessed into it in individual (non-cursive) letters. Each emblem had mounting studs that protruded through holes in the body, and to which sheet-metal speed nuts were secured to hold the emblem tightly in place.

Fender Emblems were applied in two locations: to the forward edge of the fender, above the bumper; and between the wheel opening and rear edge of the fender. "RS" or "SS" emblems (individual letters) were mounted in the forward position. V-8 models (except Z28s) were given an emblem in the rearward location, beneath a "CAMARO" block-lettered emblem. Z28s had no external identification emblems and were hard to distinguish from a base Camaro Coupe.

Grille Emblems were used on all models, and were centered on the grille. Base Camaro Coupes

Few cars on the road had an interior as pleasing as the 1967 Camaro. Whether in base form or optional Custom trim, as shown here in this well-equipped convertible, a driver and passengers rode in comfort and style without spending a fortune.

Shown here is another Custom interior, though this one features a manual transmission.

used the standard Camaro tribar logo. Super Sport models equipped with the 350 (RPO L48) engine used an emblem with the letters "SS" above the numerals "350". Grille emblems for Super Sports equipped with either of the 396-inch engines simply read "SS". Z28s did not have a unique emblem: they used the base Camaro emblem unless also equipped with the Rally Sport option, in which case the RS emblem was used. Similarly, Rally Sport models used the RS emblem unless combined with one of the SS options, in which case the appropriate "SS" emblem took precedence.

Interior

Camaro interiors were designed to offer a high degree of comfort and convenience, even in base form. The concept was simple: by making more items standard equipment, each item cost Chevrolet less money to produce than if the item were only installed optionally on a few cars.

Two basic interior trim levels were available: base and Custom (RPO Z87). The base interior was simple but attractive with all-vinyl bucket seats, vinyl-covered door panels with separate armrests, and simple emblems and controls. The Custom interior was a modestly priced upgrade that rewarded buyers with molded door panels with integral armrests, more pleasing controls, upscale emblems, and high-styled seats.

Instrument Panel
The Camaro instrument panel (IP, for short) was styled similarly to that of its sporty big brother, the Corvette, with three sections: on the left are the

This standard 1967 interior is beautiful in red, and happens to feature the N34 wood-grained steering wheel.

This 1967 model is loaded with mechanical and convenience options. Note the automatic transmission shifter and the disc brake medallion on the brake pedal, plus the console, clock, bright Custom interior, and other items.

Cars equipped with RPO C60 air conditioning featured a baseball-sized vent at each end of the instrument panel. Non-air cars had no such vents.

An auxiliary gauge panel was available under RPO U17, which was only available on V-8 models if ordered with a console. The auxiliary panel was mounted beneath the center of the instrument panel and was secured to the front of the console.

Instruments

The standard Camaro instrumentation consisted of the left gauge pod with a 120-mile-per-hour speedometer with integral idiot light windows for oil pressure, brake system pressure, and the left turn signal arrow.

The right gauge pod contained either a fuel gauge and idiot light windows (for the generator output, coolant temperature, and the right turn arrow), or an optional tachometer (the redline varied with the engine). A high-beam headlamp indicator light was located between the tops of the two gauges.

If option RPO U17 Special Instrumentation was ordered, it included a tachometer in the right pod plus an auxiliary instrument panel mounted to the console (a requirement for U17). The auxiliary panel included the following gauges: fuel level and water temperature (left pod), clock (center pod), and oil pressure and ammeter (right pod).

A close-up of the main instrument cluster (above) in a 1967 RS-SS model shows the 120-mile-per-hour speedometer and a 7,000-rpm tachometer with a 5,200-rpm yellowline and a 5,500 redline. This four-speed car has the U17 Special Instruments mounted to the underside of the dash (right), which required the D55 console.

The following list provides the tachometer redlines, by engine:

Engine	Yellow-line	Redline	Max. RPM	Scale
RPO L48 350	4,750	5,000	7,000	x 100
RPO L35 396	5,250	5,500	7,000	x 100
RPO L78 396	5,750	6,000	7,000	x 100

RPO U35 consisted of a clock and a unique housing that replaced the front portion of the console.

RPO U15 replaced the standard speedometer with one that featured an adjustable, audible alarm to alert drivers to the fact that they were exceeding their predetermined travel speed.

Switches and Controls

To the left of the instrument panel's left pod are two plastic, chrome-plated switch knobs, mounted one above the other. The top switch for the windshield wipers is operated by rotating the knob; the lower switch controls the headlamps (and headlamp doors, on RS models) by pulling the knob outward, toward the driver. Both knobs and their bezels are similar in appearance, though the bezels differ due to lettering that identified the corresponding knob's function.

The ignition switch was mounted in the instrument panel, beneath the similar-looking cigarette lighter, to the right of the steering column.

primary instruments; in the center are the heating, ventilation, and air conditioning controls (if equipped), plus the radio (if equipped) and a flip-down ashtray; on the right is the glovebox.

The instrument panel itself was constructed of sheet metal and featured a soft, vinyl-covered dash pad along the top. The panel could be body color or black.

The center section of the instrument panel features a black face panel with a bright surround.

This RS model has the rare column-mounted shifter for its automatic transmission, since the ultrarare bench seat option precluded a floor shifter. Also note the RPO U57 Stereo Tape Player mounted beneath the instrument panel.

The standard-style steering wheel used different horn buttons, depending on the model and options ordered. Here an "SS-350" emblem gives away this model's performance potential.

To the right of the right instrument pod is the cigarette lighter and the ignition switch, stacked as the wiper and headlamp switches were on the left side. The cigarette lighter has a similar appearance to the wiper and headlamp switches; the ignition switch has a similar bezel to the three switches, for a uniform appearance.

The heating, ventilation, and air conditioning controls consisted of three levers that traveled horizontally. Chrome plastic knobs capped the lever ends.

Steering Wheels

Nineteen sixty-seven Camaros were available with one of three steering wheels: the base wheel featured a three-spoke design with a black plastic rim and minimal bright trim, the Deluxe steering wheel (RPO N30) was similar to the base wheel but added bright trim along the three spokes, and, finally, RPO N34 netted the buyer a walnut-grained plastic steering wheel.

Steering Columns

Two steering columns were available. The base column, which was included on most cars, was a standard, non-tilting column that served a few different purposes: First and foremost, it transmitted steering inputs to the steering box. Second, the left side of the steering column mounted the turn signal lever switch. Third, on the column's right side is a push-pull switch that controls the hazard indicator lamps.

The Custom Interior seat (left) featured a different pattern and a bold stripe.

Lap belts were standard equipment (right). AS1 added "standard-style" shoulder belts; A85 added shoulder belts to Custom interiors; and A39 added Custom Deluxe belts front and rear (to standard interior cars).

There are two important things worth noticing in this photo: the one-year-only vent window, and the AS2 headrests for the front bucket seats.

The AL4 Strato-back bench seat (right) was installed in just 6,583 cars (out of 220,906). It was among the least expensive options at just $26.35. RPO A67 added some utility to the Camaro with a folding rear seat (below) that actually allowed the car to carry some cargo (though at the expense of passengers).

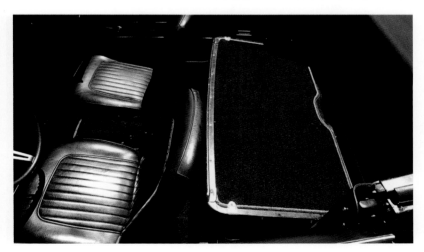

A tilt column was available under RPO N33. The tilt control lever was located just forward of the turn signal lever and was operated by gently pulling it toward the driver. The column tilted near the instrument panel and provided approximately 6 inches of wheel movement, with detents approximately every inch.

Steering columns were painted to match the instrument panel, which meant they were either body color or black.

Seats

There were several seating options for 1967 Camaros.

Base seating included vinyl-covered, low-back bucket seats up front with a matching vinyl-covered bench in the back. The seat covers were available in a number of colors to match or contrast with the body color. (See the Color and Trim Combination chart in this chapter.)

A step up the seating ladder was the RPO Z87 Custom Interior seat, which featured color-keyed accent bands on the seat bottom and seat back. The vinyl seat covers also featured a more elaborate pattern.

In a strange move by Chevrolet, a bench seat was available at extra cost by selecting RPO AL4, replacing the two front buckets.

Buyers could also add Strato-Ease headrests to their seats by opting for RPO AS2.

RPO A67 replaced the fixed rear seat with a folding version.

Seat Belts

Nineteen sixty-seven Camaros came standard with front and rear lap-type seat belts. Shoulder belts were available under RPO AS1 (standard style) or A85 (Custom). RPO A39 upgraded all lap-type belts to Custom Deluxe status. Belts and buckle receivers are color-keyed to the interior, as are retractor covers.

Door and Kick Panels

Two Camaro door panel designs were available in 1967: standard or Custom (RPO Z87). Standard panels were vinyl-covered cardboard with separate padded armrests in a matching color. Custom Interior door panels were a molded design with an integral armrest and a recessed door handle. Custom panels also featured a segment of carpeting along the bottom one-fifth of the panel.

Both door panel designs used the same door lock knobs and the same window crank assemblies. Door release handles differed between the two panel designs. Standard door release handles were long, gently curved, chrome-plated pot metal with a similar design to that of the window crank. Handles for the Custom panels were short, angular, chrome-plated pot metal that more closely resembled the exterior door handles.

Plastic kick panels were color-keyed to the rest of the interior and featured a sliding switch to control airflow through the panels' air vents.

Headliner

All 1967 Camaros use a color-keyed vinyl-like headliner. Metal support rods span across the top through stitched-in channels in the headliner to help support it. The interior of the C-pillars is covered by cardboard sail panels covered in the same headliner material. Custom Interior cars also feature small, round opera lights in the sail panels instead of the standard single dome light normally mounted in the center of the headliner.

Carpet

All 1967 Camaros feature two-piece, nylon-blend, loop pile carpet from the factory. A front piece extends from the firewall rearward to just before the front seats, where it overlaps a rear piece that covers the rest of the floor rearward, ending beneath the rear seat. On the sides, the carpet is secured by the aluminum doorsill trim plates.

Camaro carpets were available in a number of colors to match or contrast with interior trim colors. A small plastic grommet was used to provide a tidy hole around the foot-operated headlamp dimmer switch, and a plastic heel pad was dielectrically bonded to the carpet to prevent wear beneath the driver's feet.

Radios, Tape Players, Speakers, and Antennae

Two radios were offered to Camaro buyers in 1967: a monaural AM push-button radio (RPO U63) and an AM/FM push-button radio (RPO U69).

Either radio played through a single speaker, which was mounted in the center of the instrument panel, beneath a grille in the top of the dash. A second speaker was optional (RPO U80), which was mounted beneath the package shelf behind the rear seat.

The standard antenna was a fixed-mast unit mounted to the right front fender. RPO U73 was available for those who wanted an antenna mounted to the top of the right rear quarter panel.

Perhaps the most unusual option on the 1967 Camaro option list was the RPO U57 Stereo (8-track) Tape System. The system consisted of a large player unit plus four speakers. In non–air conditioned cars the unit could be installed instead of a radio, or it was available for dealer installation, which typically resulted in the unit being mounted atop the console lid.

The standard door panel (left) had a vinyl cover over a cardboard back, plus a screw-on armrest and less fancy door hardware. The molded Custom Interior door panel (below) had an integral armrest and a recessed door latch release handle. The hardware was generally improved, as was the appearance and durability.

Bright aluminum doorsill plates had both form and function. They were not only stylish and inviting, but also served to secure the front and rear sections of carpet.

The standard four-speed shifter ball was imprinted with the shift pattern.

Shown here is the underdash installation of the RPO U57 Stereo Tape Player.

Camaros equipped with a radio featured an antenna mounted to the front fender, unless RPO U73 was selected, in which case a manual antenna was mounted to the top of the right rear quarter panel, as seen here.

Console Assembly

RPO D55 added a console and floor-mounted shifter to any Camaro except those equipped with the Strato-back front bench seat (RPO AL4). The mostly plastic unit provided a storage compartment with a hinged metal lid, rear ashtray, rear courtesy light, unique seat belt stowage clips (one per side), an attractive shifter trim plate assembly, and also served as the mounting point for the RPO U17 three-gauge instrument cluster or the U35 clock. It was available in a variety of colors to match or contrast with the interior trim.

Shifters

A number of shifters were installed in Camaros during 1967. Though rarely installed, column shifters were available for those buyers who didn't want a floor-mounted shifter and were willing to stick with the base three-speed manual or two-speed PowerGlide automatic transmissions. Many optional transmissions included a floor-mounted shifter, some with or without a console.

Manual Transmission Shifters

All manual transmission shifters, whether column mounted or floor mounted, utilized rigid linkage

assemblies to convert shifter movements to engagement (or disengagement) of the various transmission gears.

RPO M11 added a floor-mounted shifter to Camaros equipped with the base three-speed manual gearbox and a six-cylinder or 327 V-8 engine. This was the same shifter included with the RPO D55 center console.

Next up the ladder was the RPO M13 heavy-duty three-speed manual transmission, which included a floor-mounted shifter.

Each of the Muncie four-speed manual transmissions—which for 1967 were the M20 and M21 units—also included floor-mounted shifters that utilized Muncie linkage. These particular units were often criticized for their imprecise action and feel. The shifter rod was a chromed steel shaft with a black plastic shift knob.

Automatic Transmission Shifter

The M35 PowerGlide automatic was supplied with a column-mounted shifter when attached to six-cylinder engines. The column-mounted shifter was a basic chromed steel rod attached to the right side of the steering column. A small black plastic knob capped the end of the rod.

V-8 engines equipped with a PowerGlide automatic received a floor-mounted shifter that consists of a chromed steel shaft and a chrome-plated T-style shifter handle with a rectangular detent-release button on its top.

The heavy-duty M40 Turbo Hydra-matic automatic, which was available for the L35 396, used a variant of the PowerGlide shifter designed to work with the three-speed transmission. While the automatic shifter worked well, it was not intended to be a performance piece.

Pedals

Camaros use either three or four foot-operated pedals, depending on the installed transmission.

Accelerator Pedal

All Camaros use a tall, slender, plastic accelerator pedal attached to a bent steel rod that is hinged on the firewall. The accelerator pedal connects to either mechanical linkages that actuate the carburetor throttle plates, or to a cable that serves the same purpose.

Brake Pedals

All Camaros use a parking brake pedal that is mounted to the underside of the instrument panel, beside the left kick panel. The parking brake pedal assembly features a small, 2-inch pedal with a ribbed rubber pedal pad that has the word "PARK" molded into it. A small release T-handle with the words "BRAKE RELEASE" is positioned above the pedal assembly, beneath the instrument panel.

All Camaros also have a brake pedal, however, the pedal assemblies are different for models equipped with a manual transmission than with automatics. Manual transmission cars use a square pedal approximately 3.5 inches wide attached to a thick steel arm suspended from the instrument panel. Automatics use a rectangular pedal roughly 6 inches across. In each case, the pedal sports a ribbed rubber cover. Cars with disc brakes have a small, round metal medallion embedded into the center of the pedal pad. The same brake pedal assemblies were used for non-assisted and power-assisted brakes; the pedal arms featured two mounting holes—one for use with power-assist systems, another for use with non-assisted (manual) brakes.

Clutch
Cars equipped with a manual transmission also have a clutch pedal, which is similar to the brake pedal assembly.

Trunk
Camaro trunks are accessed through the deck lid. The trunk itself extends forward beneath the package shelf to the back of the rear seatback. The sheet-metal trunk floor and walls were painted with a gray-and-white (early) or black-and-aqua (late) speckled paint with random dots of color, and a vinyl trunk mat with a gray-and-black houndstooth pattern was installed. Unfortunately, the mat often trapped any moisture that entered the trunk, and allowed rust to form beneath it, unseen . . . usually until it was too late and the trunk floor was ravaged by rust.

The trunk is rather featureless. The only points of interest are the spare tire, jack equipment, and lug wrench, plus optional equipment and the convertible top "cocktail shaker" vibration dampers.

Spare Tire
Spare tires were of the same size and make as those installed on the vehicle. The wheel on which the spare tire was mounted was typically a base steel wheel, and lies with the face (front) of the wheel down. The jack equipment is stowed inside and beneath the spare tire assembly.

Jack Equipment
Camaros were equipped with a multipiece set of jack equipment, which included the jack post, jack base, the ratcheting load rest bracket, the lug wrench, a screwdriver, a retaining bolt, and a wing nut.

The jack post had a cadmium-plated finish, while the load rest bracket and base were painted semigloss black; the retaining bolt and wing nut were given a zinc-oxide finish. The lug wrench was either painted semigloss black or given a zinc-oxide finish, depending on the time of year and

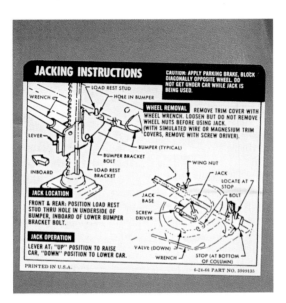

Nineteen sixty-seven Camaro trunks (above) were, like much of the car, simple but attractive. With a speckle-paint finish and a standard trunk mat, the trunks were initially easy to maintain. The spare tire, unfortunately, consumed the lion's share of the space. Jack equipment was stowed inside and beneath the spare, both to keep things together and to minimize lost space. A closer view (above left) of the stowed jack and spare shows just how things were secured at the factory. The jacking and jack-stowage instructions (left) consisted of simple illustrations in black ink on a white decal.

Chevrolet used the underside of the Camaro deck lid as a bulletin board in 1967. One decal provides jacking (and jack-stowage) instructions, while the other warns drivers and service technicians that the car is equipped with a limited-slip (C80) rear differential assembly.

manufacturing plant. Different screwdrivers were used, depending on the time of year and manufacturing plant.

Convertible Top Equipment
Convertible Top Vibration Dampers resemble large cocktail shakers, approximately 5 inches in diameter and 10 inches tall. One was installed in each corner of the car as the Camaro convertible body structure was considerably weaker than the coupe, due to the lack of the roof, so the body flexed and vibrated more. The vibration dampers were an attempt to minimize the unwanted body movements. The dampers were installed prior to the trunk being painted at the factory, so they typically feature trunk paint overspray.

Instructional Decals
A number of instructional and information decals were affixed to the underside of the Camaro deck lid. The exact number of decals varies with the specific options installed. All Camaros featured a jacking instruction decal; limited-slip Positraction differential (RPO C80) and Rally wheels (RPO P12) each added a decal to the deck lid.

Powertrain

Camaro powertrains—the engine, transmission, and rear axle assemblies—were some of the car's most desirable features, especially for performance enthusiasts. The powertrain was also largely responsible for giving a Camaro its "personality," from a mild-mannered six-cylinder economy car to a fire-breathing, big-block–powered drag strip dominator.

Many of the most sought-after Camaros are desirable because of their powertrains. Camaros such as the Z28 with its race-ready 302, and the L78 Super Sport with its 375-horsepower 396 are among the most prized Camaros to this day.

In addition, Chevrolet's legendary 350-ci small-block V-8—the most popular engine of all time—debuted exclusively in the 1967 Camaro as the cornerstone of the SS-350 package.

Engines
There were eight engines from three different engine "families" available to the Camaro buyer in 1967: two inline six-cylinder engines, four small-block V-8s, and two big-block V-8s. Power output ranged from a pedestrian 140 horsepower to nearly triple that with the L78 396.

This flexibility was afforded by the Camaro's chassis design (and most other Chevrolet models for that matter), which allowed nearly any current Chevrolet engine as long as the correct corresponding engine mount assemblies were used.

A great many individual engine parts also interchange between the different Camaro engines, and many options were available with any engine because they only required different mounting brackets. Alternators, power steering pumps, and air conditioning compressors are excellent examples of such interchangeability.

Selecting a particular engine often meant that other options were required, optional, or unavailable. For example, the L78 396 required the close-ratio M21 Muncie four-speed manual gearbox; all other transmissions were unavailable, as was RPO C60 air conditioning. Likewise, RPO Z28, which included the 302 small-block, also required a four-speed manual gearbox, disc brakes, and the coupe body. Gear ratio availability was also linked to engine selection.

I-6 Engines
Economy-minded buyers or those on a shoestring budget could still enjoy the Camaro style and excitement, albeit without the tire-shredding performance. But that was one of the beauties of the Camaro: six-cylinder models looked every bit as exciting as a Z28 or Super Sport. Just like the performance models, the six-cylinder models were offered as either a coupe or convertible, and all the same great convenience options were available.

The **Base 230**-ci inline six-cylinder was a no-frills source of 140 horsepower. With a simple single-venturi Rochester carburetor, the engine was the model of simplicity. It was cost-efficient, easy to maintain, and provided sufficient power to get your Camaro anywhere you needed to go. Still, relatively few Camaro buyers—just 17,643—opted to stick with the minimalist powerplant.

RPO L22 replaced the base 230-ci six with a mildly hotter 250-ci inline-six that churned out a whopping 155 horsepower. It provided a modest improvement in acceleration, and for the extra

$26.35 it wasn't a bad deal. But for just $100 over the base six-cylinder coupe's price, buyers could drive home in a base V-8 coupe, which was a much better deal. The 210-horsepower 327 also provided considerably more torque than either of the straight-sixes.

V-8 Small-Block Engines
The bulk of the 1967 Camaros rolled off the Norwood and Los Angeles assembly lines with a V-8 engine. Though all the performance models were V-8 based—the SS-350, SS-396s, and Z28—those cars actually accounted for only a modest percentage of all the 1967 Camaros produced. Roughly 125,000 Camaro coupes and convertibles were powered by either the base 327 or the optional 327, which provided spirited driving though hardly qualified as performance engines.

The small-block engines, dubbed "Turbo-Fire" on their air cleaner and/or rocker cover decals, were largely the same in appearance and basic equipment, except where noted in the following

descriptions. Each engine started with a cast-iron block with 4.40-inch bore centers, and all four Camaro small-blocks also featured 4-inch-diameter cylinder bores—only the crankshaft stroke varied from engine to engine. All four engines also used cast-iron cylinder heads, though different castings were used for different engines.

Internal components were largely the same for each small-block V-8, as well. Each of the 1967 Camaro's small-block engines used cast-aluminum pistons, except the Z28's 302, which used forged aluminum for higher strength. Each engine used cast-iron connecting rods of the same 5.7-inch center-to-center length, again, except the 302, which used forged-steel rods. Crankshafts were of similar cast-iron construction, excluding the 302's forged-steel crank. The 302, 327, and 350 each had different crankshaft stroke requirements: 3.00 inches, 3.25 inches, and 3.48 inches, respectively. Timing chain sets were similar for all small-blocks, and the camshafts for all but the Z28 were hydraulic grinds (lobe profiles did differ from

All new for 1967 was the 350 small-block V-8 engine, which was the centerpiece of the SS-350 performance package. The engine was a long-stroke version of the venerable 327 and would prove to be the longest-lasting version of the small-block, continuing through 1997 in the Camaro.

Another SS-350 engine, this one features the proper air cleaner lid decal. Note the chrome-plated finish on the air cleaner lid, rocker covers, and oil fill cap. The single-snorkel air cleaner base restricted airflow, but kept the engine significantly quieter.

engine to engine). The rest of the valvetrain was similar for all engines, though the Z28's engine did feature larger 2.02/1.60-inch valves.

The typical Camaro small-block V-8 used a mechanical fuel pump attached to the right side of the engine, and a Delco distributor that featured a single set of breaker points and a vacuum advance mechanism. A canister-style Delco ignition coil was painted black and mounted vertically in a black-painted sheet-metal bracket behind the carburetor. The oil pan, timing chain cover, and rocker covers were made of stamped steel. Cast-iron log-type exhaust manifolds were a cost-effective and quiet method of guiding exhaust gases to the exhaust pipes.

Most engine-driven accessories, such as the alternator, power steering pump, and air conditioning compressor, were mounted on the left side of the engine in 1967. A "short"-style water pump was used for all engines, but the fan assemblies and pulleys used for each engine varied with the engine and options ordered. Likewise, the har-

monic dampers (the crankshaft "balancer"), flywheel or automatic flex-plate, and clutch assemblies varied with the specific engine and transmission ordered.

Engine assembly took place at either GM's Flint, Michigan, or Tonawanda, New York, engine assembly plants, depending on the specific engine model. Assembled engines (less their carburetor, distributor, starter, and front-mounted accessories such as the alternator, power steering pump, and air conditioning compressor) were painted Chevrolet Engine Orange in a process that lasted roughly 30 seconds. Engines were suspended from a conveyor and moved into the paint booth, where painters hastily held "masks" to minimize overspray on exhaust manifolds and any aluminum components, such as the Z28 302's intake and rocker covers. Due to the rapid pace and inexact methods, overspray, paint runs, and even bare spots were common.

Base 327-ci engines were installed in the standard V-8 coupes and convertibles. There was very

This 350 with air conditioning and an Air Injection Reactor system (AIR) pump is installed in an RS-SS (above). The AIR pump assembly features a natural cast-aluminum case, while the steel pulley was painted 60 percent gloss black. The air conditioning compressor's steel case is 30 percent gloss black with various decals. Nineteen sixty-seven SS-350s (opposite) came with cast-iron intake manifolds and were started by a Delco top-post battery. The manifolds featured a natural finish, and although they were quickly masked with cardboard during the engine painting process, it was common for the manifolds to receive varying amounts of orange overspray.

little remarkable about the engine. A two-barrel Rochester carburetor mixed fuel with air it ingested through a single-snorkel, closed-element metal air cleaner assembly; the air mix flowed through a cast-iron intake manifold and cast-iron cylinder heads to the cylinders, where cast-aluminum pistons compressed it at an 8.75:1 ratio to produce 210 horsepower. A mild hydraulic camshaft operated iron valves that measured 1.94 inches for the intake and 1.5 inches for the exhaust. Exhaust gases exited through a standard single-outlet exhaust system, though duals were available under RPO N61 for an extra $21.10.

RPO L30 substituted a 275-horsepower 327-ci engine for the base engine. The L30 327 relied upon a 10.0:1 compression ratio and a Rochester QuadraJet four-barrel carburetor to develop its additional power, compared to the base 327. Otherwise, the two were the same, internally and externally.

RPO L48 got a buyer the 350-ci V-8 as part of the first of three Super Sport options in 1967. The first and only 350 available, the L48 was essentially a long-stroke version of the L30 327. It used the same four-barrel carburetor, cast-iron intake, heads, cam, and other parts. Compression rose slightly to 10.25:1 due to the increased cylinder volume afforded by the 350's 3.48-inch stroke, and power output was 295 horsepower at 4,800 rpm with 380 foot-pounds of torque at 3,200 rpm. The L48 came with an attractive set of chrome-plated steel rocker covers, instead of orange-painted steel.

RPO Z28 needs little description for most Camaro enthusiasts, though in 1967 it was little

known to anyone except a handful of racers. Chevy literally went out of its way not to promote the availability of RPO Z28, which added an abundance of road racing–inspired equipment. Though RPO Z28 added a number of non-engine-related components, the engine itself was a marvel. To meet the Sports Car Club of America (SCCA) 5.0-liter-displacement rules for Trans-Am competition, Vince Piggins and Corvette guru Zora Duntov combined a 350's 4.0-inch-bore block with a 283's 3.0-inch crankshaft stroke to achieve 302 cubic inches. With an aggressive mechanical cam, a 780-cfm Holley four-barrel (with vacuum-operated secondaries) atop an aluminum intake, large-valve (2.02/1.60-inch) heads, and forged-aluminum pistons that created an 11.0:1 squeeze, the Z28 302 produced 290 horsepower and 290 foot-pounds of torque. With its forged-steel crankshaft, forged-steel connecting rods, and other internal fortifications, the Z28's 302 also proved to be an excellent foundation for a race motor, as racers—and the Z28's competition—soon found out.

Unlike the Z28 302 and the L78 396, which used Holley four-barrels, most Camaro V-8s featured Rochester-built QuadraJet four-barrel carburetors, such as this one (above) on a 350. The aluminum-bodied QuadraJet features small primary venturis and massive secondaries, and originally had a goldish cadmium-plated finish. In 1967, you couldn't get much more stylish than a new RS-SS Camaro convertible (opposite). Combine drop-top fun with the tire-frying muscle of a Super Sport's V-8 and you had a car that looked great and ran even better!

Unlike other small-block V-8s, the 302 utilized an open-element air cleaner with a chrome lid. The engine could also be ordered with a unique cold-air induction system that routed outside air to the engine through a large plastic duct that drew air from the right cowl plenum. The plenum induction system, which was shipped from the factory in the car's trunk for dealer- or owner-installation, added $79 to the $358.10 Z28 package. Another ultrarare Z28 "option within an option" was the special "Cross-Ram" induction system, which utilized two 600-cfm Holley four-barrel carburetors on a boxlike aluminum intake. As the name suggested, the right carburetor fed

Mystery Engines

In addition to the engines described in this text, there is speculation that other engines may have been installed in Camaros, but those speculations have not been confirmed . . . nor definitively disproven. While you need to be skeptical whenever you come across a Camaro with a suspicious engine, you should also keep an open mind because there is evidence that several other engines were once installed or slated for installation.

The most well known of the "maybe motors" is the pair of 283-ci engines (one was coded MU for use with a Powerglide and the other, MD, would be mated to a four-speed) that Tonawanda engine production records indicate were produced. Chevrolet records don't show that any were actually installed in cars on the assembly line, but Chevrolet records aren't exactly foolproof.

The "tuner" Camaros—Yenkos, Bergers, Nickeys, and Baldwin-Motions—are widely known. It's also common knowledge that Yenko's 1969 models actually had their 427-ci big-blocks installed on the Chevy assembly lines, despite

the fact that the 427 wasn't on the option list. Those cars have become known as COPO (Central Office Production Order) Camaros.

There is compelling evidence that at least two 1968 Camaros appear to have been equipped with iron-headed versions of the L-88 427 Corvette engine. And, more recently, there has been speculation that some 1967 Camaros featured factory-installed 427s pirated from Corvette production and installed by special order for Yenko Chevrolet, as a precursor to the COPO-built cars that would come later.

It is certain that Chevrolet often built development "mules" for durability or concept testing; however, such cars were rarely made available to the general public. At least, not initially. As with the one-and-only Z/28 Convertible built for Chevy General Manager Pete Estes in 1968, some cars were built for and sold to GM executives, and later were often resold as used cars to the general public.

the left bank of cylinders, and the left carburetor fed the right bank.

The Z28 302 was also available with equal-length, tubular steel exhaust headers. Like the plenum induction system, the headers were shipped in the car's trunk. They added an extra $421.30 to the Z28's price tag.

The Z28 also featured finned aluminum rocker covers, and the pulleys installed were special deep-groove units to minimize the chance that a fan belt would be thrown at high engine speeds. Unlike other small-block V-8s, the 302 was only available with the RPO M21 close-ratio four-speed manual transmission.

V-8 Big-Block Engines
Two Mark IV big-block V-8 engines were available for 1967, both of which displaced 396 cubic inches. Altogether, 5,141 Camaros were produced with Chevrolet 396-ci V-8s for 1967.

Despite the fact that both the L35 and L78 396s were based on the L78 Mark IV 396 that

debuted in the 1965 Corvette, the two had few specific parts in common, as we'll soon cover.

RPO L35 was the code for the "low-performance" SS-396 in 1967. As such, the parts were inexpensive but durable: a cast-iron cylinder block with two-bolt main bearing caps and 4.094-inch bores; a cast-iron crankshaft with 3.76-inch stroke; cast-iron connecting rods; cast-aluminum 10.25:1-compression pistons; cast-iron cylinder heads with small, efficient "oval" intake ports; a cast-iron intake manifold with a Rochester QuadraJet four-barrel carburetor and 14-inch open-element air cleaner assembly; and a mild hydraulic camshaft. Cast-iron exhaust manifolds ushered burned gases to a standard dual-exhaust system. The L35 396 made 325 horsepower at 4,800 rpm and 410 foot-pounds of torque at just 3,200 rpm.

RPO L78, despite identical external and internal dimensions, was an entirely different engine. For starters, though it was essentially identical to the 425-horsepower L78 of 1965, Chevrolet down-rated the engine to 375 horsepower (at

The ultimate Camaro in 1967 didn't come from Chevrolet, but rather a Chevrolet dealer. Don Yenko, owner of Cannonsburg, PA–based Yenko Chevrolet, did what any good hot-rodder wanted to: he dropped a 427 Corvette engine between the Camaro's fenders.

5,600 rpm) and blamed the Camaro's more restrictive exhaust manifolds for the reduction. The L78 still used a cast-iron block with 4.094-inch bores, but four-bolt main bearing caps secured a forged-steel crankshaft (3.76-inch stroke) that swung forged-steel connecting rods fitted with 11.0:1, domed, forged-aluminum pistons. A high-lift, long-duration mechanical camshaft opened massive 2.18/1.76 valves. The heads appeared similar to the L35s, externally, but actually featured cavernous rectangular-shaped intake ports. A high-rise aluminum intake manifold fit between the heads, and a 780-cfm Holley four-barrel bolted to it. As with the Z28 302, the L78 was only available with the RPO M21 close-ratio four-speed manual transmission.

Transmissions

Camaro buyers had four manual transmissions and two automatics to pick from when placing an order.

Manual Transmissions

The base transmission was a three-speed manual unit manufactured by GM's Saginaw division. It was available with the six-cylinder and 327-ci V-8 engines. The unit featured a cast-iron case but was otherwise unremarkable.

A step up the option list from the base three-speed was the heavy-duty Warner Gear three-speed manual, available as RPO M13. Available for any engine except the 302 and L78, the M13 was the (required) base transmission for the L48 and L35 engines.

A wide-ratio four-speed transmission manufactured by GM's Muncie (Indiana) division was available as RPO M20. With its natural-finished aluminum case and fully synchronized internal gearing, the M20 was available for any engine except the Z28 302 and L78 396. The M20 had a low 2.52:1 first-gear ratio.

The final manual transmission was a close-ratio four-speed, the M21, also manufactured by GM's Muncie division. Like the M20, the M21 featured a fully synchronized gear cluster and a natural-finished aluminum case, but the M21's spread between gears was much closer, allowing an engine to better remain in its peak operating (rpm) range. The 2.20:1 first gear did make it a bit harder to launch, but the narrow spread between gears made it far superior in all other respects.

Automatic Transmissions

A two-speed automatic, known as the "Power-Glide," was available to Camaro buyers as RPO M35. Available with any engine except the Z28 302 and the 396, the PowerGlide had been around for years and was a proven, reliable shift-for-itself

The transmission of choice for most Camaro buyers was a four-speed. And for high-performance applications that meant a close-ratio Muncie (Indiana)–built box (above). Muncie four-speeds featured a natural-finish lightweight aluminum main case and tailhousing. Camaro rear axle assemblies (right) were typical of most GM Salisbury-type assemblies. Two designs were available: a low-performance "10-bolt" model, and a high-performance "12-bolt" model with a larger, stronger ring gear. All were generally painted semigloss black, while the universal joints and yokes were left natural.

You can quickly ID the rear axle assembly by the number of bolts at the bottom of the rear cover: two bolts (shown) is a heavy-duty 12-bolt; one bolt signifies a low-performance 10-bolt assembly.

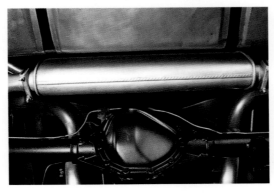

transmission that 122,727 buyers chose to pay $184.35 ($194.85 with a V-8) to add to their Camaro. PowerGlides were available with both aluminum and iron cases. Those units installed in Camaros typically had an aluminum case, though it is also possible that iron-case Power-Glides were installed.

RPO M40 was a buyer's key to the Turbo-Hydra-Matic three-speed automatic, built by GM's Hydra-matic division. The M35 was the TH400 model and was suitably strong to survive behind the L35 396, though the L78 didn't develop sufficient vacuum to operate the transmission's various servos and modulators.

Driveshafts

All Camaros utilized tubular steel driveshafts with forged-steel input and output yokes. Depending on the assembly plant, shift, and time of year, some driveshafts were painted semiflat black, while others were left natural. It's also common for the driveshafts to feature small, brightly colored paint marks that indicated the application for which that driveshaft was intended; the marks allowed for quick identification on the assembly line, as driveshafts differed in length and yoke configura-

tion depending on the transmission and rear axle assembly in a particular vehicle.

Rear Axle Assemblies

Camaros were equipped with either of two basic rear axle assemblies in 1967: a "10-bolt" assembly for most applications, or a heavy-duty "12-bolt" assembly for high-performance applications. The nicknames 10- and 12-bolt referred to the number of bolts that secured the removable rear carrier cover to the housing.

Both assemblies were available with a variety of gear ratios (dependent upon engine and transmission combinations) and with or without GM's Positraction limited-slip differential (RPO C80).

No significant parts interchanged between the 10- and 12-bolt assemblies, though they shared the same basic design. Both assemblies were typically painted semigloss black or left natural. All axle assemblies were fitted with drum brake backing plates, since no rear disc brake assemblies were available from the factory. The wheel stud bolt pattern was typical for GM: five on 4¾ inches.

Two characteristics make it easy to identify certain 1967 Camaro rear axle assemblies. First, 1967 Camaros were the only Camaros to feature

Yenko Super Camaros weren't just all substance, though—they had abundant style, too. The Stinger-style fiberglass hood was a Yenko addition, as were the Pontiac Rally wheels. This Yenko has Tuxedo Black (code AA) paint and a red standard bucket interior (code 741). Yenkos started life as L78 SS-396 models.

Perhaps one of the nicest wheels ever to roll off a Chevrolet assembly line was the original Rally wheel, shown here wrapped by a red-stripe tire. The steel wheel featured generous, oval-shaped cooling vents and bright trim rings and center caps. The wheel was standard on Super Sport and Z28 models, and optional on lesser Camaros.

rear window. Because the body structure is responsible for the structural integrity of the vehicle, rust is more of a problem on the Camaro than on a more conventionally built car such as the Chevelle, which uses a body-on-frame design.

Subframe Assembly

The front portion of the chassis is comprised of a heavy-gauge steel subframe assembly that attaches to the unibody body structure with six rubber body mounts and heavy-duty bolts. The subframe serves as the mounting structure for the front suspension and steering components, as well as the engine and transmission.

The front wheels typically produce the harshest jolts and vibrations to the passenger compartment, but with the Camaro subframe's rubber mounts, those harsh signals are dampened, which gives the Camaro the solid feel of a much larger car.

In addition, because of the subframe's heavy-gauge steel construction, it's an exceptionally strong structure to which the front suspension can be connected. A sturdy structure is essential for accurate suspension action. By contrast, the Mustang's weaker, fully unitized body construction flexes and twists when subjected to suspension forces.

Floor Pan

The Camaro floor pan is an integral part of the body structure. The floor pans are typical formed sheet-metal construction and are welded and sealed to the body structure. The floor pans contain several drain holes that are plugged with removable sheet-metal discs. During the early production process, the body structure is submerged in a chemical bath to clean it and prepare it to receive primer and paint. The drain holes allow the chemicals to more completely drain from the body assembly. The drain plugs are installed with sealant after the assembly is thoroughly dry.

Camaro floor pans generally exhibit only minor rust or corrosion unless subjected to severe conditions or neglect. Leaking door and window seals or convertible tops allow water to enter the passenger compartment and puddle up in the footwells, leading to rust formation, which can become quite severe if not treated early.

In an effort to restore some of the structural integrity forfeited by removing the hardtop on the convertible models, the floor pan was reinforced with a steel plate that spans the transmission tunnel and is secured with several screws.

Wheels and Tires

A variety of wheels and tires were available on the Camaro to enhance both its appearance and its

both rear shocks mounted forward of the axle. Second, high-performance models such as the trio of SS models and the Z28, each featured a torque arm to control axle windup and wheel hop under heavy acceleration.

Chassis

The 1967 Camaro uses a "semi-unitized" chassis construction. The combination construction offers a "best-of-both-worlds" compromise: it's cost-effective, like a unibody design, yet it's sturdy, quiet, and smooth like a body-on-frame design.

Body Structure

The passenger compartment and trunk area were built as a unibody assembly of sheet metal and pinch-welds. This method was lightweight, reasonably strong, and inexpensive. Unfortunately, the unibody assembly results in fairly poor noise, vibration, and harshness characteristics since the suspension system and a number of other components attach directly to the body structure.

The Camaro body structure is prone to rust in the typical spots: rocker panels, the bottom of the quarter panels, the trunk floor, and around the

performance. All wheels were of stamped-steel construction, in varying designs and sizes.

A number of different tire suppliers were used throughout the 1967 model year. In addition, the tires installed often varied between the two Camaro assembly plants in Norwood, Ohio, and Los Angeles, California.

Wheels
Two wheel designs were available on 1967 Camaros: the basic steel wheel with either a full wheel cover or a small "dog dish" cover for the wheel center; and the "Rally"-styled steel wheel, which featured a bright center cap and trim ring. The wheels were available in different diameters and widths, depending on the options ordered. The base wheel measured 14.0x5.5 inches. The SS options included Rally wheels that measured 14.0x6.0-inches. The Z28 received a 15.0x6.0-inch version of the Rally wheel.

Tires
A number of different tire makes, models, styles, and sizes were installed on Camaros at the two factories throughout the 1967 model year.

The majority of the tires were 7.35x14.0, including the base tires and RPO PQ2 white-stripe tires and RPO P58 whitewall tires. RPO PW6 put D70x14 two-ply red-stripe tires on a buyer's Camaro, while Z28s rolled away on 7.35x15.0 tires.

Common makes and models were Goodyear Polyglas-GT and Firestone Wide-Oval for the performance tires; Uniroyal Tiger Paws were also common.

Suspension
The suspension system is the same basic design as on many of Chevrolet's larger, established vehicles. Unequal-length upper and lower control arms with a coil spring and shock absorber in

This Granada Gold 1967 RS-SS convertible is loaded with options, including Rally wheels, rear antenna, front bumper guards, and red-stripe tires, in addition to the RS and SS packages.

Yenkos were available with any option (and then some!) that an L78 SS-396 could be ordered with. Or, as this Yenko shows, they could be ordered largely devoid of any options, which made for a better strip stormer.

between keep the front tires in contact with the ground, while a single "Monoleaf" leaf spring with vertical tube shocks was designed to keep the rear wheels firmly planted. The front suspension worked well and was durable, but the Monoleaf rear springs proved to be weak and resulted in a number of revisions being made during the model year and especially for 1968.

Front Suspension

The front suspension consists of upper and lower A-arms of unequal length. A coil spring is seated in a pocket in the lower A-arm and a deeper pocket in the underside of the frame rail. A shock absorber fits inside the coil spring and is bolted to both the frame rail and the lower control arm. A spindle is connected to both the upper and lower

control arms using pivoting ball joints. The control arms fasten to the frame rail using rubber control arm bushings.

To minimize body roll while cornering, all Camaro models were equipped with a front anti-roll bar ("sway bar"). The hollow, tubular bar features a squared-C shape and is secured to each frame rail with rubber bushings and steel brackets. Each end of the bar is connected to its respective lower control arm with a vertical mounting link consisting of a threaded bolt, various rubber bushings and washers, plus a tubular spacer and a nut.

Rear Suspension
The rear suspension of 1967 Camaros utilizes a single leaf spring per side, which Chevrolet called a Monoleaf. Each leaf featured either a natural metal finish or a semigloss black finish, depending upon how they were supplied to the assembly plants, which varied at different times of the year.

To control the spring action, shock absorbers were bolted to the spring plates, just inboard of the rear axle assemblies' brake backing plates, forward of the axle centerline. The top of each shock protrudes through the trunk floor, where a bushing and nut secure it.

Because the single-leaf rear springs were not sufficient to prevent axle windup during aggressive acceleration, performance models such as the Super Sports and Z28 were equipped with a torque rod to minimize wheel hop. The torque rod connected to a special mount on the right side axle tube and to a bracket on the chassis' integral rear subframe rail.

Nineteen sixty-seven Camaros were not equipped with rear anti-roll bars from the factory.

Brakes
While base Camaro brake systems were hardly cutting edge with their four-wheel drum assemblies, several options were available that greatly enhanced the Camaro's ability to shed speed.

The primary brake system operated on hydraulic pressure generated when the driver stepped on the brake pedal. The hydraulic fluid flowed from a natural-finish cast-iron master cylinder through natural-finish steel brake lines to a natural-finish cast-iron proportioning valve, which reduced pressure to the rear brakes to prevent them from locking the wheels during braking. Since weight transfers forward under braking, making the rear of the vehicle "light"

The Camaro was available with front disc brakes from the very start. The calipers were based on the Corvette calipers, and featured large cast-iron units with four individual pistons. The natural-finish calipers provided vastly superior stopping power, when compared to the standard drum brakes, but proved to be troublesome and leak-prone.

Nineteen sixty-seven Camaro rear axle assemblies were equipped with drum brakes, gas-charged shocks, and leaf springs. Both RPOs J56 and J65 added metallic linings to the rear drums (the former accompanied heavy-duty front discs, while the latter was in conjunction with metallic front drum linings). This happens to be a Yenko-modified Camaro, hence the reason it has a multileaf spring pack. Original 1967 models used only a single leaf per side.

would allow the rear brakes to lock prematurely and possibly cause the car to spin out of control.

The secondary brake system utilized natural-finish steel-stranded cables operated by the parking brake pedal to engage the rear brakes. The brake cables were encased in a spiral steel sheath from the firewall to a point beneath the driver's floor pan, where the single cable pulled a bracket connected to each of the rear brake cables. The rear cables have a sheath that runs from the backing plate to a bracket on the rear subframe rail.

Front and Rear Drum Brakes

Four-wheel drum brakes were standard on 1967 Camaros. The drums were not finned and featured a natural machined-metal finish. The brake shoes featured a friction material that was bonded to the steel shoe. Hydraulic wheel cylinders forced the shoes against the interior face of the drums to generate friction that slowed the car. A steel backing plate provided the necessary mounting surfaces for the wheel cylinder, various springs, and other brake system components, in addition to preventing debris (but not water) from entering the brake system.

RPO J50 added a vacuum-operated power assist to the drum brake system to reduce the brake pedal effort necessary to operate the brake system. The booster unit is a circular steel vacuum diaphragm assembly mounted between the master cylinder and the firewall. Power brake–equipped Camaros utilize different master cylinders from those without power brakes. In addition, the brake pedal assembly uses a different hinge point than non–power brake systems.

RPO J65 replaced the standard brake shoes with heavy-duty metallic linings that were better able to withstand the heat generated during braking, without fading.

Front Disc/Rear Drum Brakes

Replacing the front drum brakes with available disc brakes provided a significant improvement in braking ability. RPO J52 not only rewarded shrewd buyers with the front disc assemblies, but also a power assist system, similar to RPO J50, though with a different master cylinder and proportioning valve.

The Delco-Morain cast-iron calipers were similar to the four-piston Corvette calipers introduced and in use since 1965. Unfortunately, they also shared the Corvette calipers' tendency to leak brake fluid, due to porous cylinder walls and poor piston seals. The calipers featured a natural finish, as did the machined cast-iron rotors.

RPO J56 took the front disc/rear drum one step higher by upgrading the standard organic pads and shoes with heavy-duty front pads and metallic rear shoes. However, this option was only available in combination with RPO Z28.

Steering

Camaro steering systems are not unlike those of other Chevrolet models. Steering inputs are transferred from the steering wheel through a steering column to a recirculating-ball steering box, which converts the rotary motion into a linear motion that acts upon a series of linkages to ultimately steer the front wheels.

The steering wheels are large by today's standards: 16 inches in diameter for the standard wheel, and a similar size for the RPO N30 Deluxe wheel and the RPO N34 wood-grained wheel. The large wheel increased the driver's leverage, which reduced steering effort, but also reduced steering feel somewhat.

Steering wheel inputs traveled forward through either of two steering columns that were available: the standard, fixed-angle column, or the RPO N33 tilt column. Both columns featured a chromed turn signal stalk with a round plastic knob on the left side of the column. Tilt columns featured a shorter, but similar-looking, stalk forward of the turn signal lever to operate the tilt mechanism. Vehicles not equipped with a floor shifter featured a long chrome shift lever on the right side of the column. Both steering columns also featured a small hazard lamp switch on the right side of the column.

The steering column connected to a simple, semiflat black-finish steel steering shaft, which in turn connected to the steering box through a flexible steering coupler, more commonly known as a "rag joint."

There were several different steering boxes available, each of which mounted to the left subframe rail between the front cross-member and the firewall, and featured a natural cast-iron finish with a natural-finished aluminum access cover. Standard was a non-assisted manual unit with a 24:1 gear ratio and linkage that resulted in a 28.3:1 overall ratio. RPO N44 quick-ratio steering yielded a 21.4:1 overall ratio, while the Z/28's with RPO N44 provided a much lower 17.9:1 overall ratio for a far better feel and action at speed.

Ordering RPO N40 provided a variable-ratio, engine-driven, hydraulic power steering assist. Without RPO N44, RPO N40 featured a 16.1:1 ratio on-center (15.5:1 overall) that reduced to a 12.4:1 ratio at full-lock. The same steering box was used for cars equipped with both RPOs N40 and N44, but differences in the steering linkage resulted in a higher-effort 14.3:1 overall ratio on-center.

A natural-finish cast-iron pitman arm connected the steering box output shaft to the parallel relay rod (more commonly called a "drag link" or "center link"), which is supported at the right subframe rail by the idler arm. The ends of the relay rod connect to the inner tie-rod ends. Tie-rod adjustment sleeves connect the inner tie-rod ends to the outer tie-rod ends, which connect to the steering knuckles. The relay rod, idler arm, tie-rod ends, and steering knuckles were all natural-finished cast iron, while the tie-rod adjustment sleeves were natural-finished steel.

Fuel System

Nineteen sixty-seven Camaro fuel systems were very simple by today's standards: a fuel tank, fuel lines, mechanical fuel pump, a small in-carb fuel filter, and the carburetor. But there are differences between the systems used for six-cylinder cars, small-block V-8s, and big-block V-8s.

All cars utilized the same galvanized steel, 18-gallon fuel tank that was mounted behind the rear axle, beneath the trunk floor using two stainless-steel straps. The filler neck extends up from the rear of the tank, and then attaches to the taillamp panel behind the opening in the middle of the panel. An in-tank fuel float system, complete with a sock-type debris filter, controls the analog fuel level gauge in the instrument panel or auxiliary gauge cluster.

The natural-finish aluminum housing of a mechanical fuel pump (with a gold cadmium-plated steel diaphragm cover) is mounted to the right-hand side of the engine (all engines, I-6 through Mark IV V-8) and is operated by a steel fuel pump actuator rod, which rides against a special lobe on the camshaft. The pump draws fuel from the tank through natural-finish steel fuel lines (5/16 inch for six-cylinder and low-performance V-8s; 3/8 inch for high-performance small-blocks and both 396s) to itself, then forces it (pressure varies with rpm) through another steel line to the carburetor inlet.

Carburetor inlet ports are equipped with a sintered-bronze fuel filter, as a last defense against dirt or debris.

The specific make and model of carburetor installed on any given Camaro depended upon that vehicle's engine and other optional equipment. All six-cylinder models were equipped with a single-venturi aluminum carburetor manufactured by GMs' Rochester division. Low-performance small-blocks wore two-barrel Rochester carburetors. High-performance small-blocks (except the Z/28) and the 325-horsepower 396 were fitted with a four-barrel Rochester QuadraJet

Examples such as this 1967 RS-SS convertible, finished in Granada Gold, make it clear why the Camaro was so popular. Its body was stylish, rounded, and exciting, and the available powertrain and chassis options made it a truly exceptional performance car.

carburetor. The Z/28 and 375-horsepower 396, on the other hand, used a true racing carburetor: Holley's model 4150 780-cfm four-barrel.

Exhaust System

Camaro exhaust systems were simple and largely typical for the day: natural-finish (with some overspray near the cylinder heads) cast-iron exhaust manifolds collected gases from the engine and then funneled them to individual "header" pipes. For single-exhaust systems, the left-hand header pipe crossed between the subframe crossmember and the oil pan sump to merge with the right-hand pipe to feed the intermediate pipe. The intermediate pipe ran rearward inside the transmission tunnel and then swept up and over the left-hand side of the rear axle assembly, into a single transverse-mounted muffler. A single tailpipe exited the right-hand side of the muffler, curved rearward, and dumped the exhaust gases out beneath the rear lower valance panel.

A dual-exhaust system, such as RPO N10, was similar; however, the individual header pipes did not merge, and the system utilized two individual intermediate pipes. RPO N10 still relied upon a

single, transverse-mounted muffler, though with two inlets (one per side) and two outlets (again, one per side). The N10 tailpipes each curved rearward and exited beneath the valance panel, one on each side of the muffler.

All exhaust pipes and mufflers were natural-finished mild steel tubing and were quite prone to rusting. Header and intermediate pipe diameters were conservative: single-exhaust and small-block (except Z/28) dual-exhaust systems were comprised of pipes that measured 2.0 inches, while Z/28 and 396 dual-exhaust systems utilized 2.25-inch pipes for increased flow capacity and efficiency. Tailpipes measured 2 inches in diameter, regardless of the system.

One unique option-within-an-option was the Z/28's available tubular steel exhaust headers, which added more than $400 to the price of RPO Z28. The nearly equal-length headers were not installed at the factory, however. Instead, Chevrolet set the headers in the vehicle's trunk and left it up to the buyer to either install the headers themselves, or let the dealership do it for them.

Cooling System

Camaros were equipped with at least one of two cooling systems. The first cooling system was designed to keep the engine and drivetrain from overheating. The second cooling system was designed to do the same for the occupants of the vehicle.

Engine Cooling System

The engine cooling system used a cast-iron, engine-turned water pump to circulate coolant (a 50/50 mixture of water and ethylene glycol) through the engine block and cylinder heads. The coolant absorbed heat from the engine, and then dissipated that heat as the coolant flowed through the radiator, before beginning the cycle all over again.

An engine-turned fan assembly (mounted to the nose of the water pump) draws air through the radiator to ensure sufficient cooling capability even when the vehicle is stopped. The fan's efficiency is maximized by use of a fan shroud, which helped direct the airflow, plus provided some protection that prevented owners or would-be mechanics from accidentally coming into contact with the spinning fan blades.

A thermostat was mounted in a housing atop the intake manifold and served as a restriction to reduce coolant flow through the engine, to maintain a predetermined engine operating temperature (typically 180 degrees Fahrenheit).

A two-row radiator was used as the base radiator for six-cylinder and small-block V-8 engines, and typically was more than sufficient to keep the engine cool while running. However, high-performance models—such as the Z/28 and 396—plus options that required additional cooling capacity, including RPO C60 air conditioning or RPO V01 heavy-duty radiator (included with RPO C60), utilized "oversized" radiators. RPOs C60, V01, and Z28 were outfitted with three-row radiators. Four-row radiators were installed in Camaros equipped with 396s to cope with their demanding heat-dissipation needs. All the radiators featured copper cores and aluminum end tanks. The entire assembly was painted a semigloss black to help prevent corrosion. GM's AC division was the source for Camaro pressure caps (typically 15 pounds) that were installed to maximize efficiency.

Upper and lower radiator hoses are flexible black molded rubber and are secured to their respective bungs with natural-finish aluminum tower-style hose clamps. Heater hoses were, likewise, rubber and were secured with tower-style clamps.

A number of fans were available for installation on a Camaro, depending on the vehicle's particular cooling requirements, which were largely dictated by the options selected. The base fan,

used for most six-cylinder models and some low-performance small-block V-8s, featured four steel blades. Most small-block V-8s utilized fans with either five or seven aluminum blades, while 396s utilized only seven-blade fans. In addition to the different blade configurations, the fans were mounted to the water pump snout using either a rigid aluminum spacer or a temperature-controlled fan clutch, which disengaged at higher engine speeds to minimize drag on the engine. In all cases, the fans were painted semigloss black, while the clutch or spacer was natural aluminum.

A variety of fan shrouds were available, depending on the engine and options ordered. Two basic types existed, however. The first type was really more of a shield than a shroud: it mounted to the top of the radiator core support and prevented people from accidentally touching the fan while it rotated. The shield also featured a bold warning decal to further deter accidental contact with the fan.

The second shroud style was a true shroud that encircled the fan as it rotated, greatly improving airflow through the radiator fins, thus enhancing the cooling system's abilities. The shrouds were plastic two-piece assemblies, with an upper and lower half joined by a series of coarse-threaded sheet metal–style screws through metal retainer clips and secured to the radiator core, supported by $\frac{5}{16}$-inch fine-thread bolts.

Passenger Cooling System

The passenger cooling system came in two flavors: natural or artificial (air conditioned).

The base system was a simple ventilation system, which worked surprisingly well thanks largely to the vent window on each door. Swinging the vent window around fully directed gobs of air to the interior.

The RPO C60 air conditioning system is a bit more complex, consisting of compressors, evaporators, condensers, dehydrators, and other assorted components.

The compressor is a cylindrical, semigloss black object driven by a belt turned by an engine pulley. It's mounted on the right-hand side of the engine by a series of brackets and spacers. The compressor features a bright-red metallic ID plate with the word "Frigidaire" and system maintenance specifications.

The condenser is a natural-finished aluminum, radiator-like component attached to the core support just forward of the radiator. As with a radiator, the "coolant" (called "R12" or better known as "Freon") in the air conditioning system passes through the condenser to dissipate the heat it has absorbed during the process of cooling the interior air.

Chapter 2
1968 Camaro

Identification

While the 1968 Camaro looks remarkably similar to the 1967 models, there are a number of readily visible identifiers that differentiate the two model-year vehicles, plus a key change to the official, legal identification—the Vehicle Identification Number (VIN) plate.

Whereas the 1967 VIN plate was mounted to the forward door pillar, and was only visible with the door open, in 1968 the VIN plate was relocated to the top of the instrument panel, visible through the windshield.

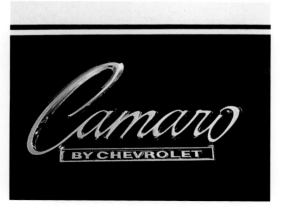

The Camaro entered its second year greatly refined, which made the Camaro a far better car to own, to drive, and to race. This is a 1968 SS-396 with the top-option 375-horsepower L78 396 V-8. Note the lack of vent windows, the revised parking and directional signal lamps in the updated grille, and the new SS side striping.

Camaro spotters have several visual clues that distinguish a 1968 from a 1967 model. The lack of vent windows is, perhaps, the most obvious change for 1968. Second would be the addition of side marker lamps, front and rear. Front turn signal indicator lamps also changed from round to semi-rectangular on non–rally sport (RS) models, though RS models still utilized square lamps in the lower valance. Out back, 1968 Camaro taillamps were segmented visually into two segments per assembly by a redesigned bezel.

Additional exterior changes for 1968 included updated striping options, revised emblems and emblem placement, and a subtle restyling of the grille assembly. For more information, see the Body section.

Several changes were also made to 1968 Camaro interiors, including new seats, steering wheels, a new console design, revised instrumentation, and more. See the Interior section for more information on these changes.

Last, but not least, were changes under the 1968 Camaro's hood. An additional 396 was added to the lineup, and various alterations were made to other engines, the available transmissions, rear axle assemblies, and other aspects of the chassis equipment, including brakes and suspension.

Although the 1967 and 1968 Camaro models look remarkably similar, the 1968 is a much more refined automobile and a better performance car.

Vehicle Identification Number (VIN)

The vehicle identification number (VIN, for short) is used to legally identify and differentiate the vehicle from any other on the road. For 1968, the Camaro's VIN tag changed somewhat in design and its location. The tag was moved from the 1967 location—on the driver's door hinge pillar—to the base of the windshield, inset into the top of the instrument panel, on the driver's side. The 1968 VIN tag is also smaller than in 1967, measuring roughly 1/2 inch by 2 1/2 inches. And although still made of tin, the tag is painted flat black to minimize glare when being viewed from outside the vehicle. As in the past, the characters are stamped into the tag from beneath, resulting in raised characters. The tag no longer featured the word "CHEVROLET", as in the past, since that information was already coded into the VIN itself.

For information on how to decode Camaro VIN tags, refer to Appendix A.

Trim Data Tag

The 1968 trim tag is virtually identical to the 1967 version, and unlike the VIN tag, continued to be affixed to the upper left cowl (firewall) panel, inside the engine compartment, adjacent to the windshield wiper motor. The original purpose of

the tags was to identify the specific vehicle's body style, original paint treatment, interior trim equipment, and specific accessories for service repair purposes. The tags also contain coded data to represent when the vehicle was "built" (the week of assembly) and the plant at which it was assembled. For information on how to read 1967 Camaro Trim Data Tags, please refer to the accompanying illustration.

For information on how to decode Camaro trim tags, please refer to Appendix B.

The 1968 VIN tag was relocated to the top of the instrument cluster to make it visible to law-enforcement officials.

Body trim tags were, again, installed on the firewall, as in 1967. The aluminum tag was riveted to the firewall prior to painting, so it received the same 30 percent gloss-black paint as the firewall. The trim tag identifies the date the body was assembled, the color(s) it was scheduled to be painted, the trim level and color for the interior, and also listed certain options that affected the vehicle's assembly as it moved down the production line.

Engine Stamping

VIN and data tags were not nearly as all-inclusive as modern vehicle information decals, which list not only the VIN and trim data, but also Regular Production Option (RPO) codes for options included on the vehicle.

One critical shortcoming of the old VIN and trim tag systems was that neither precisely identified the exact engine that the vehicle was supposed to have installed underhood. General Motors (GM) partially overcame this shortcoming by stamping the engine model and partial VIN into a flat, machined pad along the front of the engine.

The stamping consisted of two sets of characters and numbers. The first set utilized a two-letter code to identify the engine "model," plus the assembly date and plant information. The second set of characters was a partial VIN sequence that matched the engine assembly to the specific vehicle. Thus, the engine can be positively identified as a particular model (such as a Z28's 302), and positively linked to the vehicle, which helps to certify that a particular vehicle was equipped with a specific performance package (or not). The catch to engine stampings is that they are often machined off when an engine is rebuilt (specifically, when the cylinder case deck surfaces are milled), and false codes can be restamped.

General Recognition Info

Apart from the "official" identification each Camaro has—VIN, trim tag, engine stampings, and so on—there are a number of other ways to identify a 1968 model from a distance.

The first thing to determine is that a particular vehicle is, in fact, a first-generation (1967–1969) Camaro. Most enthusiasts will have little trouble doing this, though from a distance, 1970–1971 Plymouth Barracudas and Dodge Challengers do bear more than a passing resemblance to Chevy's original pony car.

Of the three years that comprise the first-generation Camaro era, the 1969 models look considerably different due to all-new sheet metal that year (for more information on the specific characteristics of 1969 models, please refer to chapter 3, which covers them in detail). Discerning a 1967 model from a 1968 is less simple, because only fairly subtle differences exist between the two.

From the sides, you get two distinct clues. First, 1968 Camaros have one-piece side windows, in contrast to the vent windows in conjunction with retractable windows used in 1967. Second, 1968 Camaros were the first Camaros to be equipped with side marker lamps.

Identifying a 1968 Camaro from the front can be a bit more challenging. The easiest thing to look for is the turn signal lamps: rounded rectangular units are mounted in the grille, inboard of the headlamps on non–Rally Sport models. Nineteen sixty-eight Rally Sport Camaros continued to be equipped with square marker lamps located in the lower valance panel—just like the 1967 models. The only difference is the grille, which for 1967 is composed of numerous small squares versus the rectangles used for 1968.

All first-generation Camaros have a similar appearance from the rear, as well. However, there are subtle clues to help you distinguish a 1967 from a 1968 from a 1969. The most obvious differences all involve the taillamp assemblies. Nineteen sixty-seven and 1968 assemblies are nearly identical, while 1969 units are much wider. Nineteen sixty-seven taillamp bezels are a simple, rectangular-shaped chrome surround with the inside area of the bezel painted semi-gloss black. Nineteen sixty-eight units, although similar, have a vertical rib that divides each taillamp into two halves.

Chassiswise, 1967 and 1968 Camaros again appear very similar. The most "noticeable" change was the relocation of the left rear shock absorber's lower mounting point to a position rearward of the axle centerline, resulting in a "staggered" shock layout (the right shock continued to be mounted ahead of the axle centerline) that helped reduce axle windup under hard acceleration, which minimized wheel hop. The change eliminated the need for the auxiliary torque arm installed on 1967 performance models.

Again, as in 1967, many major Camaro components—engine, transmission, axle housing, frame rails, body structure, and so on—continued to be stamped with VIN-based identification numbers, simplifying the authentication process.

1968 CAMARO PRODUCTION FIGURES

RPO	Description	Units
12337	Camaro sport coupe (6-cyl)	53,523
12337	Camaro sport coupe (6-cyl)	47,456
12367	Camaro convertible (6-cyl)	3,513
12437	Camaro sport coupe (V-8)	167,251
12467	Camaro convertible (V-8)	16,927
L34	Super Sport package w/350-hp 396-ci V-8	2,579
L35	Super Sport package w/325-hp 396-ci V-8	10,773
L48	Super Sport package w/295-hp 350-ci V-8	12,496
L78	Super Sport package w/375-hp 396-ci V-8	4,575
Z22	Rally Sport package	40,977
Z28	Special Performance package	7,199*

* includes one Z28 convertible

Body

The 1968 Camaro looked unlike anything else on the road . . . except the 1967 Camaro, that is. But sharing the same great design as the 1967 Camaro was hardly a detriment: the car was highly attractive and very popular with buyers. For 1968, subtle changes refined the Camaro's appearance.

Two body styles continued to be available: a coupe and a convertible, both of which shared nearly all of the same body panels, from the entire front clip (fenders, hood, header panel, valance, and cowl panel) to doors, deck lid, taillamp panel, and rear lower valance. In addition, despite subtle changes to fenders and quarter panels to accommodate marker lamp assemblies, all 1967 and 1968 body panels are interchangeable.

Body Styles

The Camaro was once again available in two body styles: a semifastback two-door coupe, and a similar-looking two-door convertible. Color palettes and combinations varied slightly from 1967; refer to the accompanying color combination chart.

Hoods

As in 1967, two basic Camaro hoods were available. The first was a basic, flat steel hood with a subtle center crease running the length of the hood from front to rear; Super Sport (SS) models were equipped with the second, similar hood, which also featured a squarish raised section to which pot metal grille inserts were fitted. While 1967 models utilized two different grille insert designs, a single design was used in 1968, regardless of the engine installed: the 1967 "stack"-style design, which had been used only on 1967 SS-396 models.

Grille Assemblies

Though they featured revised patterns, two grille assemblies remained available in 1968: one for non–Rally Sport models, and one for RS-equipped models.

The standard (non-RS) grille featured a more rectangular pattern and a noticeably more pronounced "V" shape, which resulted in headlamp assemblies that appeared to be more recessed than in 1967.

The Rally Sport grille assembly appeared very similar to the 1967 version. One significant, but invisible, change was the replacement of 1967 RS electric headlamp door motors with vacuum-operated actuators to open and close the doors.

Front Bumper

The 1968 Camaro front bumper remained unchanged from 1967: a chromed steel bumper is

1968 (EARLY) CAMARO COLOR AND TRIM COMBINATIONS

		INTERIOR TRIM COLORS AND RPO CODES						
		Black	Blue	Gold	Red	Turq	Parch./Black	Black/White
Vinyl Bucket, Standard Int.		712	717	722	724			
Vinyl Bench Opt., Standard Int.		713	718	723				
Vinyl Bucket, Custom Int.		714	719	721	725	726	730	
Vinyl Bench Opt., Custom Int.		715	720			727		
Cloth Bucket Opt., Houndstooth								749t
EXTERIOR PAINT AND RPO CODES								
RPO	Color	Stripe(s)						
A A	Tuxedo Black	White	X	X	X	X	X	X	X
C C	Ermine White	Black	X	X	X	X	X	X	X
D D	Grotto Blue	White	X	X				X	X
E E	Fathom Blue	White	X	X				X	X
F F	Island Teal	White	X					X	X
G G	Ash Gold	Black	X		X			X	X
H H	Grecian Green	Black	X					X	X
K K	Tripoli Turquoise	Black	X				X	X	X
L L	Teal Blue	White	X	X				X	X
N N	Cordovan Maroon	White	X			X		X	X
P P	Seafrost Green	Black	X		X			X	X
R R	Matador Red	White*	X			X		X	X
T T	Palomino Ivory	Black	X		X			X	X
V V	Sequoia Green	White	X		X			X	X
Y Y	Butternut Yellow	Black	X		X			X	X

*Marina Blue and Bolero Red Camaros equipped with Black vinyl or convertible tops received Black stripes. Convertible tops were available in White, Black, or Medium Blue with any exterior color. Vinyl tops were available in Black or Light Fawn with any exterior color.

1968 (LATE) CAMARO COLOR AND TRIM COMBINATIONS

		INTERIOR TRIM COLORS AND RPO CODES						
		Black	Blue	Gold	Red	Turq	Parch./Black	Black/White
Vinyl Bucket, Standard Int.		712	717	722	724			
Vinyl Bench Opt., Standard Int.		713	718	723				
Vinyl Bucket, Custom Int.		714	719	721	725	726	730	
Vinyl Bench Opt., Custom Int.		715	720			727		
Cloth Bucket Opt., Houndstooth								749t
EXTERIOR PAINT AND RPO CODES								
RPO	Color	Stripe(s)						
C C	Ermine White	Black	X	X	X	X	X	X	X
D D	Grotto Blue	White	X	X				X	X
F F	Island Teal	White	X					X	X
G G	Ash Gold	Black	X		X			X	X
J J	Rallye Green	White	X					X	X
K K	Tripoli Turquoise	Black	X				X	X	X
L L	Teal Blue	White	X	X				X	X
N N	Cordovan Maroon	White	X			X		X	X
O O	Corvette Bronze	Black	X					X	X
P P	Seafrost Green	Black	X					X	X
R R	Matador Red	White*	X			X		X	X
U U	Le Mans Blue	White	X	X				X	X
V V	Sequoia Green	White	X		X			X	X
Y Y	Butternut Yellow	Black	X		X			X	X
Z Z	British Green	White	X		X			X	X

(January 1968 Revision)
*Marina Blue and Bolero Red Camaros equipped with Black vinyl or convertible tops received Black stripes. Convertible tops were available in White, Black, or Medium Blue with any exterior color. Vinyl tops were available in Black or Light Fawn with any exterior color.

The base Camaro front end was obviously related to the 1967 model, but featured enough updates to be distinctively new. The grille features a more pronounced "V" shape plus a more rectangular pattern, while the parking lamps (which do double-duty as turn signals) were given a rounded rectangular shape. This car's "cowl induction" hood is incorrect; that hood style was not introduced until 1969.

rigidly mounted to brackets connected to the sub-frame rails. The optional RPO V31 vertical bumper guards, likewise, are the same as in 1967: chromed steel with a rubber rub strip. The exact placement of the bumper guards appears to have varied from shift to shift and assembly plant to assembly plant; however, the most widely accepted positioning has the guards attached just outboard of the license plate.

Rear Bumper
Like the front bumper, the 1968 Camaro rear bumper is unchanged from 1967's chromed steel unit, which wraps around the sides of the car. The RPO V32 rear bumper guards continued to be available, and are also identical to the 1967 guards, with their chromed steel base and black rubber rub strip.

Sides
Sheet metal on the 1968 Camaro is interchangeable with the 1967 panels; however, 1968 fenders and quarter panels do have provisions for side marker lamps, which makes the panels unique to

each year (though good bodymen have often modified 1967 panels for use on 1968 models, and vice versa).

Again, only the quarter panel design differed between coupe and convertible models; the other panels were interchangeable. Each fender and quarter panel design featured subtle flares that accentuated the wheel openings. In addition, a pronounced crease delineated the upper body from the lower.

Several options added bright trim moldings to the wheel openings, the rocker panel, and even the A-pillars, between the front windshield and the side window glass. RPO Z21 added bright trim to the wheel openings and roof drip rails (except convertibles). RPO Z22 added bright trim along the top of the rocker panel, the fender, and the quarter panel. RPO Z23 added bright trim to the A-pillars.

RPO Z21 continued to include paint accent stripes, in addition to the bright trim. For more information about stripes, see "Stripes and Body-side Moldings" later in this chapter.

Roof

Three types of roofs remained available on 1968 Camaros: painted steel, vinyl-covered steel, and convertible.

Since two-tone paint options were not available, painted steel roofs were always body color. Drip rails were body color unless a vinyl top was ordered. Vehicles not equipped with a vinyl top, but equipped with either RPO Z21 or Z22, were treated to bright drip rail moldings. Convertible models did not feature drip rails.

Vinyl roof covers were glued to a semifinished steel roof. The vinyl covers consisted of four to six individual pieces of vinyl material: a large center section that covered the bulk of the roof; one piece per side that covered the C-pillars and approximately the first 8 inches of the sides of the roof; a fourth piece was used below the rear window and stretched approximately halfway to

the deck lid along the filler panel; and, unless RPO Z23 was ordered, the A-pillar windshield posts were each covered by a sheet of vinyl. (RPO Z23 provided trim that covered the A-pillar posts.) Bright trim was used to secure the ends of the vinyl along the drip rail, along the bottom of the C-pillars, and across the deck lid filler panel. Vinyl roofs were available in black or off-white to match or contrast with the vehicle's paint color.

Convertible tops were available in three colors: black, medium blue, and white. The top material was a canvas fabric with a sewn-in clear vinyl rear window. The top's framework was primarily steel, and was available in either manual or power-operated configurations. The forward edge of the roof was secured to an oversized windshield header trimmed in bright metal by two latches. Where the top met the body panels on the sides and rear of the car, bright metal trim secured the fabric to the body.

RS models (this car also features SS equipment) were, again, the same as in 1967, but thanks to revised emblem placements and other subtle touches, were fresh looking. Note the front spoiler, which Chevy termed an "auxiliary valance" and offered as part of RPO D80. Opposite you can clearly see the "stack"-style hood louvers of the SS hood, which were used for all SS models in 1968, not just those equipped with a 396.

1968 CAMARO MONTHLY PRODUCTION

	1968 Models				
	Los Angeles			Norwood	
Month	Start	End		Start	End
August (08)				300001	301000
September (09)	300001	304745		301001	319989
October (10)	304746	309652		319990	337720
November (11)	309693	315860		337721	352898
December (12)	315861	321968		352899	368090
January (01)	321969	328091		368091	382800
February (02)	328092	331484		382801	392000
March (03)	331485	335251		392001	407303
April (04)	335252	338564		407304	426000
May (05)	338565	342086		426001	448000
June (06)	342087	345432		448001	462500
July (07)	345433	349164		462501	484735

Figures courtesy of the United States Camaro Club   (Note: Monthly start/end units are approximate)

Glass/Windows

Nineteen sixty-eight Camaro windows were, again, manufactured by Libby Owens Ford and remained easily identifiable thanks to their "LOF" and "Safety Flo-Lite" etching marks. In addition, the windows feature date-coding that makes it possible to determine the originality of the window.

Tinted windows were available under RPO A01 (all windows) and A02 (windshield only). Electrically operated power side windows were available under RPO A31.

The windshield is laminated safety glass, which breaks on impact but does not shatter.

The side and rear windows are safety plate glass, which shatters on impact.

The windshield and rear window are secured to the vehicle with a ropelike bead of black adhesive. Bright metal trim attaches to anchors

Unlike the SS models, the Z28 came standard with a base Camaro hood, albeit one painted with broad, bold stripes in a color that sharply contrasted with the body color. The stripes continued onto the cowl panel, with over-spray beneath it from paint that went through the vents. Also note the sharp "V" angle of the grille assembly, as compared to the nearly flat 1967 grille.

secured to the window channel and fills the gap between the glass and the window channel, covering the trim and minimizing the amount of debris that can enter the window channel and cause water drainage problems.

The side windows are moveable: the door's side windows—which no longer featured the vent windows used in 1967—slide up and down vertically within channels; quarter windows tilt downward along a channel concealed within the quarter panel.

A rear window defroster was available via RPO C50 and consisted of a blower motor mounted to the underside of the rear package shelf that utilized a grille mounted to the top of the shelf. When activated by the switch on the instrument panel, the motor circulated warm air from within the passenger compartment against the rear window.

Mirrors

Like the 1967 models, 1968 Camaros came with both a rearview mirror mounted inside the vehicle, hung from a support connected to the windshield header, and an outside rearview mirror, mounted toward the front of the driver's door on a chrome-plated pot metal stand. One slight difference was that the outside rearview mirror was rectangular in shape, rather than round, as in 1967. An outside rearview mirror was not available for the passenger's door.

The driver's outside rearview mirror was available in a remote-control version, which utilized a

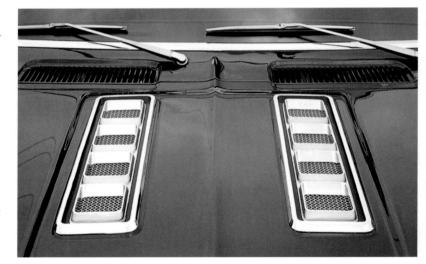

miniature joysticklike control lever and a complex assembly of cables to tilt and swivel the mirror. The remote-control system was available as RPO D33.

Headlamps

All 1968 Camaros utilized two large, round sealed-beam headlamp units; one lamp was mounted to each side of the grille. Original-equipment lamp units were supplied by Guide and are identifiable by a triangle shape cast into the center of the lens with "T-3" in its center.

Unless Rally Sport equipment (RPO Z22) was ordered, the headlamp units were exposed at all times, and were surrounded by a metal bezel.

The 1968 SS hood was unchanged from 1967, however, Chevrolet began standardizing on just a single vent style: the four simulated "stacks" per grille insert. Some early-1968 SS-350 models were reportedly built with the 1967 small-block rib-style inserts.

The door handle and door lock cylinder assembly were the same chromed, pot metal units as in 1967. Note that the D90 sport striping (which was included with the Super Sport options) ends in a dulled tip beneath the lock cylinder assembly.

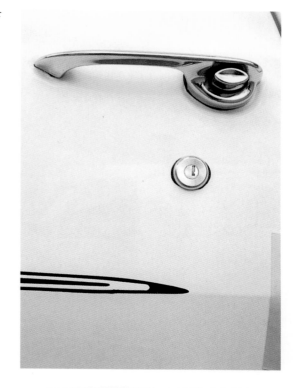

The exterior rearview mirror was changed from round to rectangular in 1968, though the base remained similar to the 1967 model.

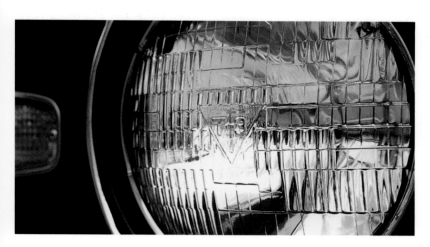

When RPO Z22 was ordered, the headlamps were concealed (when not in use) behind new vacuum-operated doors (instead of the electrically operated doors of 1967) that rotated around the center axis of the headlamp unit, and stowed beside the headlamp, toward the center of the vehicle. The headlamp doors featured a metal framework with a black plastic cover that matched the grille design. When the headlamp doors were closed, hiding the headlamps, the 1968 Camaro front end featured a clean, menacing appearance. While the change to vacuum-operated doors was hoped to end the problem of the 1967 doors' electric motors, the vacuum-driven doors also proved unreliable, due to their complexity of hoses and diaphragms that often leaked.

Taillamps

Taillamp designs were revised subtly for 1968: the chrome bezel now featured a vertical divider bar that gave the impression that each taillamp was actually comprised of two individual lamp units—an inner and an outer.

Two taillamp designs remained in use for 1968, depending on whether or not Rally Sport equipment (RPO Z22) was ordered. For non-RS cars, the outer taillamp lenses were red rounded rectangles, while the inner lenses were mostly opaque white lenses.

Rally Sport models still used solid red inner and outer lenses, since the back-up lamps were separate assemblies mounted beneath the bumper in the rear valance panel.

Bezels were also painted semigloss black on RS models, except for the outer edge, which remained chrome plated.

In either case, the taillamp assemblies served as taillamps, brake lamps, and turn signals. Non-RS models also provided backup lamp functions.

The lamp assemblies were set into the metal taillamp panel and were each trimmed with a chromed pot metal bezel. The bezels were secured from within the trunk using sheet-metal nuts that screwed onto posts cast into the bezel.

Taillamp lenses are date-coded and have a code identifying their intended use. The taillamp assemblies use only clear bulbs.

Turn Signals

As with 1967 taillamp assemblies, two front turn signal lamp designs were utilized in 1968. The first design was for non-RS models and featured rounded, rectangular lamp assemblies mounted in the

Nineteen sixty-eight Camaros, like most GM vehicles, were equipped with Guide T-3 headlamps, which are easily identified by the triangular-shaped insignia embossed into the center of the lens, and the "T-3" lettering.

grille, inboard of the headlamps. The lamps used amber or yellow-colored bulbs and clear lenses.

Rally Sport models, on the other hand, used square turn signal assemblies recessed into the outboard ends of the lower front valance panel. Again, the lamp assemblies featured clear lenses and amber or yellow bulbs.

Marker Lamps
Side marker lamps were introduced on the 1968 Camaro. The front marker lamps are small, rectangular units with clear lenses and either clear or amber bulbs. The rear lamps are the same, but feature red lenses. Both the front and rear lamps feature a chrome-plated bezel.

Back-up Lamps
The back-up lamps are, again, integral with the taillamp assemblies on non–Rally Sport Camaros, as in 1967. A rounded rectangle of translucent plastic was inset into the inboard section of each taillamp assembly. A clear bulb was used.

Rally Sport models again feature separate back-up lamps mounted beneath the rear bumper, in the rear valance panel. A translucent plastic

This 1968 RS-SS convertible shows that the RS front end changed little from 1967. The headlight doors for 1968, however, changed to a vacuum-operated system (from electrical) to improve operation and reliability. The rear of the Camaro (opposite) was similarly updated for 1968. The taillamp assemblies were given new trim rings that visually divided each lamp assembly into two pieces. Spoilers (rear and front) were more popular in 1968, as well. The SS package included a blacked-out rear taillamp panel on 396 models, as in 1967—which was a quick way to identify whether you were at least losing to a big-block SS or not.

The standard Camaro taillamp assembly for 1968 was similar to that of 1967, but was updated with a new bezel that visually segmented each taillamp into two individual lamps. The outboard lamp was always red and illuminated for braking and turn signals. The inboard lamp of non-RS models has a translucent white lens to serve as the backup lamp.

lens is mounted inside a chrome-plated metal bezel that adds a stylish touch to the assemblies.

Fuel Filler Cap

The fuel filler neck is located in the center of the taillamp panel, as on 1967 Camaros. The standard gas cap now featured the Chevrolet "bow tie" logo. Super Sport models were given a cap with "SS" initials on it. Rally Sport models were equipped with a cap with "RS" initials, unless also equipped with Super Sport equipment, in which case the "SS" cap was used. Z28 models used the standard Camaro cap, unless Rally Sport equipment was included, in which case the "RS" cap was used. Z28 models could never be equipped with the "SS" cap, as the models were mutually exclusive.

Deck Lid

All 1968 Camaros utilized the same deck lid assembly as 1967 models, regardless of body style or options. The assembly is largely rectangular in shape, and rather flat and featureless. It featured two large hinges at its forward edge. A "Camaro" script emblem was secured to the deck lid's right rear corner.

Deck Lid Spoiler

RPO D80 front and rear spoilers debuted in 1968. In order to mount the spoilers, holes were drilled through the deck lid and the spoiler's mounting studs protrude through those holes. Sheet-metal speed nuts are used to secure the spoiler to the deck lid.

RS models have red inboard lenses that duplicate the functionality of the outboard lamp. Back-up lamps on RS models are mounted in the lower valance panel, beneath the bumper.

Standard Camaros and 350-powered SS Camaros, by comparison, featured a body-color taillamp panel. But any buyer could add optional equipment such as the RPO D80 Auxiliary Panel and Valance, which gave any model a racy appearance, such as this base convertible model. The standard 1968 Camaro rear end (left) is simple and attractive. Note the Chevrolet "bow tie" emblem on the gas cap, in the middle of the taillamp panel. This car also features the RPO D80 rear spoiler, which Chevrolet called an "auxiliary panel".

The rear of the 1968 RS-SS models was also only slightly different from the 1967 RS models. The RS back-up lamps were mounted in the rear lower valance, beneath the bumper. Like all 1968 models, the taillamps had the appearance of four individual taillamps, thanks to the new bezels. On RS models, all "four" lenses are red. Non-RS models have clear translucent white lenses in the inboard spots. Super Sport models (right) featured a flat-black taillamp panel (except on black cars, which retained a glossy body-color taillamp panel) and "SS" gas cap emblem.

On vehicles that were equipped with RPO Z28 and D80 spoilers, the spoiler was installed prior to application of the stripes, so the area beneath the spoiler did not have striping paint.

In addition to the highly visible rear spoiler, the front spoiler was mounted to the bottom of the front valance balance, and was molded from black plastic. Thin metal support rods extend from the ends of the spoiler to the bottom of the front fender extension panel.

Stripes and Bodyside Moldings

As in 1967, a number of different striping treatments were applied to 1968 Camaros, from simple pinstriping along the sides to the broad, bold stripes applied to the hood and deck lid of Z28s.

Pinstripes were applied to the sides of Camaros ordered with RPO Z21 Style Trim Group or RPO Z22 Rally Sport equipment. A dual stripe began near the top of the front fender and followed the length of the fender, along the top of the door, and then along the top of the quarter panel.

Front Accent Band was Chevrolet's name for the "bumblebee stripe," available as RPO D91, that wrapped around the front of the car, starting at or slightly above the bumper line on each fender, running up the fender (breaking temporarily for any model identification emblems, usually "RS" or "SS"), and onto the front header panel, just forward of the hood. The stripe band was actually three stripes: a broad solid band in between two thin pinstripes. Unlike 1967, the D91 front accent band was no longer applied as part of the Super Sport packages, which now received the somewhat similar RPO D90 "sport stripes."

Sport Stripes, which were listed under RPO D90, were included with the Super Sport options. The sport stripes resembled the D91 stripes, in that they spanned across the header panel and down the sides of the fenders. However, halfway down the fender (beside the headlamp), the stripe turned rearward and shot backward, ending in a rounded point near the rear of the door. Again, the stripe was actually three stripes: a bold center "main" stripe, plus pinstripes that outlined the main stripe (and actually joined at the point, on the door).

"Z28" Stripes were referred to as "special paint stripes" under RPO Z28's description and were said to be applied to the hood and rear deck. In truth, the two broad (14.7-inch) stripes started on the front header panel (forward of the hood), ran back along the hood, onto the cowl panel between the hood and the windshield, skipped the roof, and then resumed on the rear deck filler panel and along the deck lid itself. The stripes were each trimmed by a pinstripe that started on one side, wrapped around the end of the stripe,

A rare, optional turn signal indicator mounted atop the front fender (above). The units were part of RPO U46, the Light Monitoring System, which was installed on just 1,755 units. Like the Corvette system, U46 relied on high-tech fiber-optic cables to transmit light from a given lamp to the monitor. New for 1968 were government-mandated side marker lamps (left), such as this front-fender-mounted unit. Note the clear lens and yellow (or amber) bulb, and the chrome-plated bezel. The rear marker lamps (left) were similar to the fronts, however, they used a red lens with a clear bulb, per government regulations.

This "Camaro By Chevrolet" deck lid emblem installed on a 1968 Camaro equipped with the RPO D80 spoiler but without the Z28 stripes indicates that either this is not a Z28 or it is a stripe-delete Z28.

A closer look at the side stripe shows how the manufacturing techniques often resulted in imperfect stripes. Assembly-line workers taped paper stripe templates to the car, then shot the paint. They rarely had the time to make sure the templates lined up properly.

and then continued down the other side of the main stripe. At the factory, special "masks" were used to prevent paint from being applied where emblems were secured on the deck lid. While the stripes were a part of RPO Z28, they could be deleted by simply noting so on the order sheet.

Window Moldings consisted of bright metal trim surrounding the windshield and rear window of all 1968 Camaros.

Lower Bodyside Moldings were included with RPO Z22 Rally Sport equipment. The bright metal trim attached along a body accent crease just above the rocker panel. Three pieces were used per side: one on the rear portion of each front fender, a second piece along each door, and the third on the front portion of the rear quarter panel.

Wheel Opening Moldings were installed on cars ordered with RPO Z21 or RPO Z22. The moldings were bright metal.

Roof Drip Rail Moldings were also part of options RPO Z21 (Style Trim Group), RPO Z22 (Rally Sport equipment), and RPO Z23 (Special Interior Group). These bright metal moldings could be installed on any coupe but were not installed on convertible models.

Vinyl Roof Moldings were installed to secure the edges of the vinyl material. Bright metal moldings were secured to the base of the A-pillar, along the roof drip rail, along the base of the C-pillar, and along the deck lid filler panel. Windshield and rear window trim was used to secure the fabric in those areas.

Door Edge Guards, RPO B93, remained a popular and inexpensive way to protect the rear edge of the doors from scratches and paint chips that could result from the occasional bump against another car or a wall.

Vinyl Bodyside Molding continued to be available as a dealer-installed option. Available in several colors to match or contrast with the car's paint color, the adhesive-backed trim was applied to the midbody crease along the side of the vehicle, on the rear of the front fender, the door, and the front of the rear quarter panel.

Emblems and Graphics

A variety of different emblems and graphic decals were used on 1968 Camaro models, depending upon the model and options ordered.

Header Panel and Deck Lid Emblems underwent a fundamental change for 1968. While the large script emphasized "Chevrolet" in 1967, such honors went to the model's name, "Camaro," in 1968. Chevrolet was still promoted, inset into a small rectangular bar beneath the Camaro script.

Fender Emblems were applied in two locations: to the forward edge of the fender, above the bumper; and between the wheel opening and rear edge of the fender. The forward location—with one notable exception—was used for engine displacement identification for V-8 models. Early Z/28s adhered to this convention with their "302" emblems, but after a few months they were replaced by "Z/28" emblems.

The rearward location, behind the wheel opening, was reserved for model identification (except the Z/28, as just noted). For base, SS, and Z/28 models, a "Camaro" script, similar to that used in the header and deck lid emblems, was mounted just above the midbody crease. Super Sport models also featured "SS" lettering beneath the crease, though base and Z/28 models had no additional emblems. Rally Sport models received unique "rally sport" lowercase lettering in place of the "Camaro" script, but no additional emblems

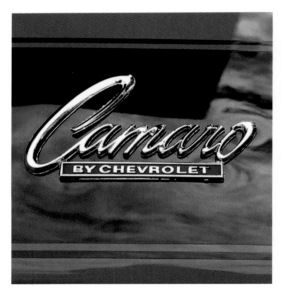

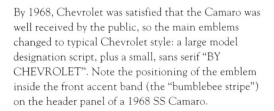

By 1968, Chevrolet was satisfied that the Camaro was well received by the public, so the main emblems changed to typical Chevrolet style: a large model designation script, plus a small, sans serif "BY CHEVROLET". Note the positioning of the emblem inside the front accent band (the "bumblebee stripe") on the header panel of a 1968 SS Camaro.

Rally Sport models received an attractive "RS" emblem in the center of the grille, instead of the base Camaro emblem. However, if combined with Super Sport equipment, the "SS" emblem took precedence on the grille. RS-Z28 combos retained the "RS" grille emblem.

This non-RS 1968 Z28 shows the proper rear stripe configuration. The stripes, which are the same width as the front stripes, do not run completely to the rear window, but rather end on the deck lid filler panel. Also note that cars equipped with D80 rear spoilers had their stripes applied after the spoiler was installed, thus the stripe is applied to the spoiler, but not to the deck lid beneath it. By comparison, cars with dealer-installed spoilers, which are identical to D80 spoilers, are applied over an already-painted deck lid, so the stripes are beneath the spoiler, and the dealer had to apply stripes to the spoiler, as well.

When applying Z28 stripes at the factory (right), a special template was used to mask the area beneath the deck lid emblem, which allowed the entire deck lid emblem to sit atop body-color paint, rather than have half of the emblem on the stripe and half on the body-color paint. Stripes on the 1968 Z28's front end (below right) were applied to three panels: the header panel (ahead of the hood), the hood, and the cowl panel. Note how the stripes wrap beneath the panels and even continue slightly on the underside of the panel, indicating that some panels (such as the header panel) were painted off the vehicle, while others (such as the cowl) were painted on the car, as indicated by the paint overspray in the cowl plenum area.

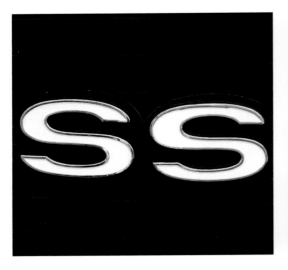

Super Sport models received an "SS" emblem on the grille (far left), whether or not the car had RS equipment. Engine designations were moved to the front of the fender in 1968, as this "350" emblem shows (left). However, there were exceptions: Z28 models started the year with "302" emblems at the leading edge of the fender, but finished with "Z/28" emblems. Some RS models featured only "RS" emblems on the fenders.

were installed in conjunction with the "RS" emblem. RS-SS combinations utilized the "SS" ornamentation only, while RS-Z/28 combinations utilized the "RS" identification convention.

Grille Emblems were used on all models, and were centered on the grille. Base Camaro Coupes continued to use the standard Camaro tribar logo. In a change from 1967, all 1968 Super Sport models received an "SS" emblem whether they were 350s or 396s. There were no more "SS350" emblems. Again, Z28s did not have a unique grille emblem; they used the base Camaro emblem unless also equipped with the Rally Sport option, in which case the "RS" emblem was used. Similarly, Rally Sport models used the "RS" emblem unless combined with one of the SS options, in which case the "SS" emblem took precedence.

Interior

At first glance, little changed about the 1968 Camaro interior. But for those who know what to look for, there are actually an abundance of changes that differentiate a 1968 interior from a 1967.

Again, two trim levels were available: base and Custom (RPO Z87). The base interior was simple, but attractive, with all-vinyl bucket seats, vinyl-covered door panels with separate armrests, and simple emblems and controls. The Custom interior was a modestly priced upgrade that rewarded buyers with molded door panels with integral armrests, more pleasing controls, upscale emblems, and high-styled seats.

Instrument Panel
The Camaro instrument panel remained similarly styled to that of its sporty big brother, the Corvette, with three sections: on the left are the primary instruments; in the center are the heating, ventilation, and air conditioning

The Camaro's "396" emblems were always set into the "SS" side striping, because both the emblems and the stripes were included as part of the Super Sport options. Also note the blacked-out SS grille. Non-SS grilles were largely a dull silver color.

While Z28s built early in the model year received "302" emblems on their fenders, later models were adorned with the famous "Z/28" emblem seen here.

Between the wheel opening and the door, 1968 Camaros received a "Camaro" script emblem, similar to that used on the front header panel and the rear deck lid. Cars equipped with RPO Z22 Rally Sport equipment replaced the "Camaro" script with a block-lettered "rally sport" emblem.

Rally Sport models defied convention and used a "rally sport" block-lettered emblem on the rear of the fender (above), instead of the "Camaro" script emblem used on all other models. With the front of the fender reserved for the engine-displacement identification, the rear of the fender (below) featured the "Camaro" script plus bold "SS" ornamentation below.

controls (if equipped), plus the radio (if equipped) and a flip-down ashtray; on the right is the glovebox. One significant change for 1968 was the addition of "Astro Ventilation," which added a round cooling vent with a ball-shaped flow director to each end of the instrument panel.

The instrument panel itself was constructed of sheet metal and featured a soft, vinyl-covered dash pad along the top. The panel could be body color or black.

The center section of the instrument panel features a black face panel with a bright surround.

The RPO U17 auxiliary instrument panel was redesigned for 1968, but continued to be mounted to the front of the floor console.

Instruments

Standard Camaro instrumentation consisted of the left gauge pod with a 120-mile-per-hour speedometer and integral idiot light windows for oil pressure, brake system pressure, and the left turn signal arrow.

The right gauge pod contained either a fuel gauge and idiot light windows (for the generator output, coolant temperature, and the right turn arrow) or an optional tachometer (redline varied with engine). A high-beam headlamp indicator light was located between the tops of the two gauges.

If option RPO U17 (Special Instrumentation) was ordered, it included a combination tachometer and clock (dubbed the "tick-tock-tach") in the right pod, plus an auxiliary instrument panel mounted to the console (a requirement for U17). The auxiliary gauges were arranged in a "sawtooth" fashion, with two rows that each contained two rectangular-faced instruments. The included instruments were fuel level, water temperature, oil pressure, and ammeter.

RPO U35, which was included in RPO U17 but was also available without it, added an analog clock to the right gauge pod. Without RPO U17, the clock was the sole instrument in the right gauge pod; with RPO U17, the clock was inset into the center of the tachometer.

RPO U15 somehow continued for 1968, though it proved even less popular, with under 2,500 buyers selecting it (compared to nearly 4,000 the year before). U15 replaced the standard speedometer with one that featured an adjustable audible alarm to alert drivers to the fact that they were exceeding their predetermined travel speed.

Switches and Controls

To the left of the instrument panel's left pod are two plastic, chrome-plated switch knobs, mounted one above the other. Windshield wipers are controlled by rotating the top knob; the headlamps (and headlamp doors, on RS models) are controlled by pulling the lower knob outward,

toward the driver. Both knobs and their bezels are similar in appearance, although the bezels differ due to lettering that identifies the corresponding knob's function.

To the right of the right instrument pod is the cigarette lighter and the ignition switch, stacked as the wiper and headlamp switches were on the left side. The cigarette lighter has a similar appearance to the wiper and headlamp switches, while the ignition switch has a similar bezel to the three switches, for a uniform appearance.

The heating, ventilation, and air conditioning controls consisted of three levers that traveled horizontally. Chrome plastic knobs capped the lever ends.

Steering Wheels

Nineteen sixty-eight Camaros were available with any of three steering wheels: the base wheel featured a three-spoke design with a black plastic rim and minimal bright trim; the Deluxe steering wheel (RPO N30) was similar to the base wheel but added bright trim along the three spokes; and, finally, RPO N34 netted a buyer a walnut-grained plastic steering wheel.

Nineteen sixty-eight Camaro interiors remained stylish yet affordable, as this convertible model shows. Note the optional Custom trim level, the teak wheel, and the automatic transmission. Shown left is a close-up of the U17 auxiliary gauge cluster, arranged in a saw-tooth-type arrangement.

Instrument panels (IPs) tell a lot about a Camaro. This particular IP tells us the car is (or originally was) a 1968 SS-396 with the L78 396. Tachometers are often an excellent indicator, thanks to engine-specific yellow- and redline markings. Speedometers, such as this car's 120-mile-per-hour unit, are less specific, though special 140-mile-per-hour speedometers were used on some models, such as those equipped with COPO 9737, the Sports Car Conversion.

Nineteen sixty-eight RS-SS interiors (above) exhibited the epitome of style, especially when equipped with a few options, such as the teak wheel and Special Interior. Standard steering wheels (right) were adorned with a model-appropriate horn button, such as the "SS" unit on this 1968 SS.

Steering Columns

Two steering columns were available. The base column, which was included on most cars, was a standard, non-tilting column that served a few different purposes: First and foremost, it transmitted steering inputs to the steering box. Second, the left side of the steering column mounted the turn signal lever switch. Third, on the column's right side is a push-pull switch that controls the hazard indicator lamps.

A tilt column was available under RPO N33. The tilt control lever was located just forward of the turn signal lever and was operated by gently pulling it toward the driver. The column tilted near the instrument panel and provided approximately 6 inches of wheel movement, with detents approximately every inch.

Steering columns were painted to match the instrument panel, which meant they were either body color or black.

Seats

Seating options changed somewhat in 1968. The base seats were still "Strato-Bucket" buckets up front, with a bench-style seat in back. Like the 1967 seats, upholstery for the base, low-back seats was a high-grade vinyl, which was again produced in a number of colors to match or contrast with the body color.

A front bench seat was kept on the option list, under RPO AL4, and was called the "Strato-back" seat. Upholstered in all-vinyl, the Strato-back bench seat wasn't a popular choice for Camaro buyers in either 1967 or 1968. Just 6,583 benches were sold in 1967, and only 4,896 in 1968.

Returning for 1968 was RPO AS2, the Strato-Ease head rests. Though a wise purchase, at $52.70, the headrests proved appealing to just 2,234 buyers—down slightly from the 2,342 buyers in 1967.

The big change for 1968 came with the new high-back front bucket seats with integral headrests, which buyers received by checking option Z87, the Custom Interior.

A step up the seating ladder was the RPO Z87 Custom Interior seat, which featured color-keyed accent bands on the seat bottom and seat back. The vinyl seat covers also featured a more elaborate pattern.

RPO A67 replaced the fixed rear seat with a folding version.

Seat Belts

Nineteen sixty-eight Camaros came standard with front and rear lap-type seat belts. Shoulder belts were available under RPO AS1 (standard style) or A85 (Custom). RPO A39 upgraded all lap-type belts to Custom Deluxe status. Belts and buckle receivers are color-keyed to the interior, as are retractor covers.

Door and Kick Panels

Two door panel designs continued to be available in 1968: standard or Custom (RPO Z87). The standard panels were vinyl-covered cardboard with separate padded armrests in a matching

The standard bucket seats (above) feature a simple vinyl covering with a plain pattern. This car is also equipped with the D55 center console. The 1968 high-back bucket seats were adorned with a Camaro emblem (left) in the integrated headrest. Note this seat's houndstooth fabric insert.

color. The Custom Interior door panels were a molded design with an integral armrest and a recessed door handle. Custom panels also featured a segment of carpeting along the bottom one-fifth of the panel.

Both door panel designs used the same door lock knobs and the same window crank assemblies. The door release handles differed between the two panel designs. The standard door release handles were long, gently curved, chrome-plated pot metal with a similar design to that of the window crank. Handles for the Custom panels were short, angular, chrome-plated pot metal that more closely resembled the exterior door handles.

The plastic kick panels were color-keyed to the rest of the interior and featured a sliding switch to control airflow through the panels' air vents.

The Special Interior seats (above) received a bold contrasting stripe, a different cushion contour, and a richer ribbed pattern. Standard 1968 door panels (below) changed little from 1967, featuring a simple vinyl cover and a separate armrest that was secured to the panel. By contrast, the Custom Interior's molded door panel (bottom) was a considerable improvement, with its integrated armrest, recessed door release handle, and more upgraded pattern.

Headliner

As in 1967, 1968 Camaros use a color-keyed, vinyl-like headliner. Metal support rods span across the top through stitched-in channels in the headliner to help support it. The interior of the C-pillars is covered by cardboard sail panels covered in the same headliner material. Custom Interior cars also feature small, round opera lights in the sail panels instead of the standard, single dome light normally mounted in the center of the headliner.

Carpet

All 1968 Camaros feature two-piece, nylon-blend, loop pile carpet from the factory. A front piece extends from the firewall rearward to just before the front seats, where it overlaps a rear piece that covers the rest of the floor rearward, ending beneath the rear seat. On the sides, the carpet is secured by the aluminum doorsill trim plates.

Camaro carpets were available in a number of colors to match or contrast with interior trim colors. A small plastic grommet was used to provide a tidy hole around the foot-operated headlamp dimmer switch, and a plastic heel pad was dielectrically bonded to the carpet to prevent wear beneath the driver's feet.

Radios, Tape Players, Speakers, and Antennae

The same radios and related equipment were available in 1968 as in 1967, with one new addition: the RPO U79 AM-FM stereo radio, which joined the RPO U63 monaural AM push-button radio and RPO U69 monaural AM/FM push-button radio.

The U63 and U69 radios played through a single speaker, which was mounted in the center of the instrument panel, beneath a grille in the top of the dash. A second speaker was optional (RPO U80), which was mounted beneath the package shelf behind the rear seat.

RPO U79 played through dual speakers, one mounted in each kick panel behind a unique mesh grille. A multiplex amplifier was mounted higher in the dash. One limitation of RPO U79 was that it was not available with the RPO U80 rear speaker; however, if combined with the U57 8-track system, the stereo system employed four speakers—the two front speakers in the kick panels, plus two more in the rear package tray.

The standard antenna was a fixed-mast unit mounted to the right front fender. RPO U73 was available for those who wanted an antenna mounted to the top of the right rear quarter panel.

Nineteen sixty-seven's RPO U57 Stereo (8-track) Tape System survived into 1968. The system consisted of a large player unit plus four speakers. In non–air conditioned cars the unit could be installed instead of a radio, or it was available for dealer installation, which typically resulted in the unit being mounted atop the console lid.

Console Assembly

RPO D55 was again available in 1968, however, it was completely redesigned to provide additional storage space and to better integrate the RPO U17 auxiliary gauge cluster. The new console design continued to be made largely of textured plastic and was color coordinated to the vehicle interior.

Shifters

A number of shifters were installed in Camaros during 1968. Though rarely installed, column shifters were available for those buyers who didn't want a floor-mounted shifter and were willing to stick with the base three-speed manual or two-speed PowerGlide automatic transmissions. Many optional transmissions included a floor-mounted shifter, some with or without a console.

Manual Transmission Shifter

A new "manual" transmission was added to the 1968 option list: RPO MB1's Torque-Drive unit. The Torque-Drive transmission was a two-speed PowerGlide that had been modified for clutchless manual shifting. It was only available with six-cylinder engines, so its application was limited; still, 3,099 buyers were intrigued enough to order the $68.65 option.

All manual transmission shifters, whether column mounted or floor mounted, utilized rigid linkage assemblies to convert shifter movements to engagement (or disengagement) of the various transmission gears.

RPO M11 added a floor-mounted shifter to Camaros equipped with the base three-speed manual gearbox and a six-cylinder or 327 V-8 engine. This was the same shifter included with the RPO D55 center console.

Next up the ladder was the RPO M13 heavy-duty three-speed manual transmission, which included a floor-mounted shifter.

Each of the Muncie four-speed manual transmissions—M20, M21, and the new heavy-duty M22—also included floor-mounted shifters that utilized Muncie linkage. These particular units were often criticized for their imprecise action and feel. The shifter rod was a chromed steel shaft with a black plastic shift knob.

Automatic Transmission Shifter

The M35 PowerGlide automatic was supplied with a column-mounted shifter when attached to six-cylinder engines. The column-mounted shifter was a basic chromed steel rod attached to the right side of the steering column. A small, black plastic knob capped the end of the rod.

All console-mounted shifters for automatic transmissions featured a new "stirrup"-style shifter, which consisted of two chromed vertical posts and a cross-handle with a detent-release button beneath it.

The heavy-duty M40 Turbo Hydra-matic automatic, which was available for the L35 396, used a variant of the PowerGlide shifter designed to work with the three-speed transmission. While the automatic shifter worked well, it was not intended to be a performance piece.

Pedals

Camaros use either three or four foot-operated pedals, depending on the installed transmission.

Accelerator Pedal

All Camaros use a tall, slender, plastic accelerator pedal attached to a bent steel rod that is hinged on the firewall. The accelerator pedal connects to either mechanical linkages that actuate the carburetor throttle plates, or to a cable that serves the same purpose.

Brake Pedals

All Camaros use a parking brake pedal that is mounted to the underside of the instrument panel, beside the left kick panel. The parking brake pedal assembly features a small, 2-inch pedal with a ribbed rubber pedal pad that has the word "PARK" molded into it. A small release T-handle with the words "BRAKE RELEASE" is positioned above the pedal assembly, beneath the instrument panel.

All Camaros also have a brake pedal, however, the pedal assemblies are different for models equipped with a manual transmission than with automatics. Manual transmission cars use a square pedal approximately 3.5 inches wide, attached to a thick steel arm suspended from the instrument panel. Automatics use a rectangular pedal roughly

Radio-delete instrument panels were little different from those with a radio. A simple filler panel took the place of the radio.

6 inches across. In each case, the pedal sports a ribbed rubber cover. Cars with disc brakes have a small, round metal medallion embedded into the center of the pedal pad. The same brake pedal assemblies were used for non-assisted and power-assisted brakes; the pedal arms featured two mounting holes—one for use with power-assist systems, another for use with non-assisted (manual) brakes.

Clutch
Cars equipped with a manual transmission also have a clutch pedal, which is similar to the brake pedal assembly.

Trunk

Camaro trunks are accessed through the deck lid. The trunk itself extends forward, beneath the package shelf, to the back of the rear seatback. The trunk was painted in a gray speckled paint with random dots of color, and a vinyl trunk mat with a gray-and-black houndstooth pattern was installed. Unfortunately, the mat often trapped

any moisture that entered the trunk, and allowed rust to form beneath it, unseen, usually until it was too late and the trunk floor was ravaged by rust.

The trunk is rather featureless. The only points of interest are the spare tire, jack equipment, and lug wrench, plus optional equipment and the convertible top "cocktail shaker" vibration dampers.

Spare Tire
Spare tires were of the same size and make as those installed on the vehicle. The wheel on which the spare tire was mounted was typically a base steel wheel, and lies with the face (front) of the wheel down. The jack equipment is stowed inside and beneath the spare tire assembly.

New for 1968 was RPO N65, the "Space-Saver" spare tire and wheel. The wheel was a fairly typical steel wheel, however, the tire was a unique design that collapsed accordion-style when not inflated, yet remained securely seated to the wheel's bead area. An "aerosol"-like canister was used to inflate the tire when it was necessary, but

The center section of the 1968 Camaro (right) was available with a simulated woodgrain panel when equipped with RPO Z23 Special Interior. Also note the woodgrain treatment on the new-style console and the new stirrup-style automatic shifter. The redesigned console (far right) went equally well with a manual shifter. Note the new RPO U17 auxiliary gauges.

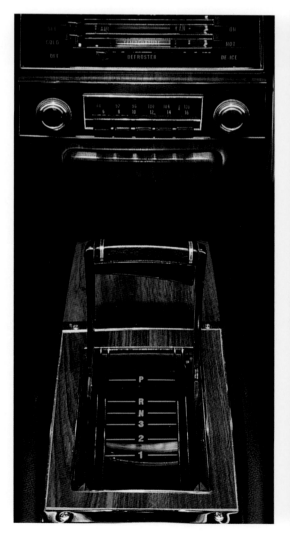

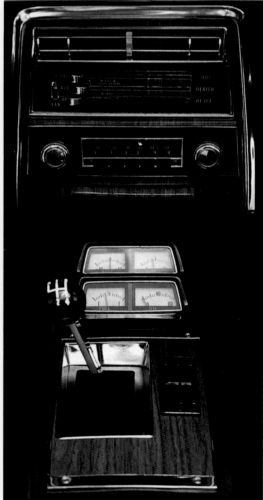

otherwise the space-saver option provided a much more compact spare tire assembly, which left much more room for packages in the trunk.

Jack Equipment

Camaros were equipped with a multipiece set of jack equipment, which included the jack post, jack base, the ratcheting load rest bracket, the lug wrench, a screwdriver, a retaining bolt, and a wing nut.

The jack post had a cadmium-plated finish, while the load rest bracket and base were painted semigloss black and the retaining bolt and wing nut were given a zinc-oxide finish. The lug wrench was either painted semigloss black or given a zinc-oxide finish, depending on the time of year and manufacturing plant. Different screwdrivers were used, depending on time of year and manufacturing plant.

Convertible Top Equipment

Convertible Top Vibration Dampers resemble large cocktail shakers, approximately 5 inches in diameter and 10 inches tall. One was installed in each corner of the car because the Camaro convertible body structure was considerably weaker than the coupe, due to the lack of the roof, so the body flexed and vibrated more. The vibration dampers were an attempt to minimize the unwanted body movements. The dampers were installed prior to the

trunk being painted at the factory, so they typically feature trunk paint overspray.

Instructional Decals

A number of instructional and information decals were affixed to the underside of the Camaro deck lid. The exact number of decals varies with the specific options installed. All Camaros featured a jacking instruction decal; limited-slip Positraction differential (RPO C80) and Rally wheels (RPO P12) each added a decal to the deck lid.

Powertrain

By 1968, the Camaro had already become a legendary performance car. Central to much of the Camaro's performance reputation was its stellar line of powerhouse engines. In 1968, the Camaro's engine line changed slightly from 1967 offerings with the addition of two 396s—the L34 350-horsepower version and the L89 396 with its lightweight aluminum cylinder heads.

Engines

The two new 396s brought the Camaro's total to 10 for 1968, again representing three different engine families: two inline six-cylinder engines, four small-block V-8s, and four big-block V-8s. Power output ranged from a pedestrian 140 horsepower to nearly triple that with the L78 396.

The trunk of the 1968 Camaro contained the standard spare wheel and tire, jacking equipment, and a decorative trunk mat.

I-6 Engines

Again, the base and optional inline six-cylinder engines provided the economy-minded buyer with excellent choices for spirited, though thrifty, driving.

Base 230-ci inline six-cylinder engines soldiered on with 140 horsepower. The engine remained essentially unchanged from 1967, from its single-venturi Rochester carburetor to its single exhaust. With so many excellent optional engines to pick from, however, fewer than 10 percent (22,322 of 235,147 units) of the 1968 Camaros were constructed with the least powerful and least costly engine.

RPO L22 remained the step-up six-cylinder engine with its 155 horsepower. Chevy enticed 28,647 buyers to shell out the additional $26.35 for the extra 15 horsepower, despite the fact that the base 327 continued to be a better deal by adding 135 horsepower for just $105 above the base six-cylinder coupe price.

V-8 Small-Block Engines

Of the 184,178 Camaros powered by V-8 engines in 1968, the vast majority—165,979—were equipped with a small-block V-8, displacing either 302, 327, or 350 cubic inches. While the Z28's 302

was, in fact, a high-performance powerplant, the 327 and 350 models provided exciting, though hardly exceptional, performance.

The small-block engine assemblies were outwardly identical in 1968 to their 1967 counterparts, though certain internal changes do make some parts exclusive to their respective years and engine sizes. For example, crankshaft journal sizes were increased beginning in 1968; however, not every engine received the stronger, larger journal sizes—not even every engine of a given displacement.

Base 327-ci engines were installed in the standard V-8 coupes and convertibles. There was very little remarkable about the engine. A two-barrel Rochester carburetor mixed fuel with air it ingested through a single-snorkel, closed-element, metal air cleaner assembly; the air mix flowed through a cast-iron intake manifold and cast-iron cylinder heads to the cylinders, where cast-aluminum pistons compressed it at an 8.75:1 ratio to produce 210 horsepower. A mild hydraulic camshaft operated iron valves that measured 1.94 inches for the intake and 1.5 inches for the exhaust. Exhaust gases exited through a standard single-outlet exhaust system, though duals were available under RPO N61 for an extra $21.10.

Central Office Production Orders

Chevy had two systems for placing orders: the Regular Production Option system and the Central Office Production Order: RPOs and COPOs, for short. Most option codes you hear about, including Z28, Z22, C60, D80, and M22, are RPOs and are available to anyone (though sometimes they are only available in conjunction with other options). COPOs, on the other hand, often had to be ordered in large quantities (several vehicles at one time). Furthermore, they weren't available directly to the public. In fact, Chevrolet didn't even want the general public to know about COPO cars, though you probably don't go a day without seeing one in public, since the primary use of the COPO system is to order police cars, taxicabs, and municipal vehicles. For police cars, COPO options add special suspension, heavy-duty cooling packages, heavy-duty electrical systems, and even special-order paint colors and schemes. For taxicabs, heavy-duty seat springs are a COPO specialty. For municipal vehicles (such as your local fire chief's car), COPO options allow for non-standard colors and factory installation of radio equipment or even specially sized wheels and tires.

In the case of Camaros, the COPO system allowed GM to install everything from entire engines to special-duty suspension components, revised instrumentation, and other components.

Three COPO codes are generally associated with Camaros: 9560, 9561, and 9737. COPO 9560 netted a buyer the ultraexotic, all-aluminum ZL-1 427 engine, plus appropriate suspension modifications and required braking and steering system upgrades. COPO 9561 was similar but featured a more "civilized" 425-horsepower cast-iron L72 Corvette 427. COPO 9737 was the "Sports Car Conversion" and was used in conjunction with the other two COPO codes. Option 9737 replaced a number of standard components with higher-performance equivalents including thicker front stabilizer bars, faster 140-mile-per-hour speedometers, and E70x15 Goodyear Wide Tread GT tires on steel 15x6 Rally wheels.

Ultimately, however, Chevrolet made no effort to promote the availability of the COPO options, as the cars were truly intended for racers only. As a result, just 69 Camaros were equipped with the $4,160.15 COPO 9560 option, while records indicate that only 1,015 L72 engines were built for the $489.45 COPO 9561 option, many of which had to be "reserved" for warranty replacements.

Today, the COPO system has been replaced with a less-covert Special Equipment Option (SEO) system, which is used by law enforcement agencies to order specially prepared Camaros for highway patrol use.

RPO L30 substituted a 275-horsepower 327-ci engine for the base engine. The L30 327 relied upon a 10.0:1 compression ratio and a Rochester Quadra-Jet four-barrel carburetor to develop its additional power, compared to the base 327. Otherwise, the two were the same, internally and externally.

RPO L48 got a buyer the 350-ci V-8 as part of the first of three (L48, L34, and L78) Super Sport options in 1967. The first and only 350 available, the L48 was essentially a long-stroke version of the L30 327. It used the same four-barrel carburetor, cast-iron intake, heads, cam, and other parts. Compression rose slightly to 10.25:1 due to the increased cylinder volume afforded by the 350's 3.48-inch stroke, and power output was 295 horsepower at 4,800 rpm with 380 foot-poundsof torque at 3,200 rpm. The L48 came with an attractive set of chrome-plated steel rocker covers, instead of orange-painted steel.

RPO Z28 needs little description to most Camaro enthusiasts, though in 1967 it was little

known to anyone except a handful of racers, and the option was only slightly more popular in 1968. Chevy literally went out of its way not to promote the availability of RPO Z28, which added an abundance of road racing–inspired equipment. Though RPO Z28 added a number of non-engine-related components, the engine itself was a marvel. To meet the Sports Car Club of America (SCCA) 5.0-liter-displacement rules for Trans-Am competition, Vince Piggins and Corvette guru Zora Duntov combined a 350's 4.0-inch-bore block with a 283's 3.0-inch crankshaft stroke to achieve 302 cubic inches. With an aggressive mechanical cam, a 780-cfm Holley four-barrel (with vacuum-operated secondaries) atop an aluminum intake, large-valve (2.02/1.60-inch) heads and forged-aluminum pistons that created an 11.0:1 squeeze, the Z28 302 produced 290 horsepower and 290 foot-pounds of torque. With its forged-steel crankshaft, forged-steel connecting rods, and other internal fortifications, the

The most popular engine in 1968 was the 350 small-block V-8, shown here. Like all Chevy V-8s, the engine was painted orange. An open-element air cleaner assembly presented little impediment to air ingestion, which aided power production. This Camaro also features air conditioning, the compressor for which is visible on the left-hand side of the engine.

By 1968, the Z28 had already made a name for itself in both drag and road racing, despite just 602 units sold in 1967. Nineteen sixty-eight Z28 production swelled to 7,199 units. This is a late-1968 model, as indicated by the "Z/28" emblem on the front fender; early models featured a "302" engine ID emblem, as in 1967. Note that the RPO D80 front and rear spoilers were not included or required with RPO Z28.

Z28's 302 also proved to be an excellent foundation for a race motor, as racers—and the Z28's competition—soon found out.

Unlike other small-block V-8s, the 302 utilized an open-element air cleaner with a chrome lid. The engine could also be ordered with a unique cold-air induction system that routed outside air to the engine through a large plastic duct that drew air from the right cowl plenum. The plenum induction system, which was shipped from the factory in the car's trunk for dealer- or owner-installation, added $79 to the $358.10 Z28 package. Another ultrarare Z28 "option within an option" was the special "Cross-Ram" induction system, which utilized two 600-cfm Holley four-barrel carburetors on a boxlike aluminum intake. As the name suggested, the right carburetor fed the left bank of cylinders, while the left carburetor fed the right bank.

The Z28 302 was also available with equal-length, tubular steel exhaust headers. Like the plenum induction system, the headers were shipped in the car's trunk. They added an extra $421.30 to the Z28's price tag.

The Z28 also featured finned aluminum rocker covers, and the pulleys installed were special deep-groove units to minimize the chance that a fan belt would be thrown at high engine speeds. Unlike other small-block V-8s, the 302 was only available with the RPO M21 close-ratio four-speed manual transmission.

V-8 Big-Block Engines
On paper, the number of Mark IV big-block engines doubled from two to four in 1968: the L34, L35, L78, and L89 396s. In reality, two of the engines—the L78 and the L89—were essentially identical, except the L89's heads were cast of

aluminum rather than iron. In addition, the L34 was an L35 with a slightly more aggressive camshaft (and different spark plugs). So, while the options doubled, from a manufacturing perspective there were still basically just two engines.

As in 1967, the 396s were only available as part of an SS package.

Though you won't find it on Chevy's option lists, Chevrolet did, in fact, build a number of 1968 Camaros with a fifth Mark IV V-8: the awesome 425-horsepower L-88 Corvette 427. The L-88, which was much like the L89, but with larger-cylinder bores and higher compression, was not available as a Regular Production Option. Instead, you had to know what you wanted and your dealer had to be willing to put through the paperwork for a Central Office Production Order (COPO). For more information on Chevrolet's COPO system, see Appendix C.

In the case of the L88 427-powered 1968 Camaros, they were produced for a select few of Chevrolet's more performance-minded dealers, including Yenko Chevrolet, Nickey Chevrolet, and Berger Chevrolet. The dealers, in turn, either

raced the cars themselves or sold them to racers who then campaigned them, and made a good showing for Chevy in the process—which helped sell more Camaros to racing fans.

RPO L34 was new for 1968 and included a 350-horsepower version of the L35 engine, plus all the usual Super Sport equipment: heavy-duty suspension, SS hood, SS emblems, SS striping (unless stripe-delete was requested), and bright engine trim. The $368.65 option was selected by 2,579 buyers.

RPO L35 was a holdover option from 1967 and featured the same "low-performance" 325-horsepower 396 and other SS parts as it did the year before. It was a bargain at just $263.30, at least that's apparently what 10,773 buyers felt.

RPO L78 didn't change for 1968. But with 375 horsepower and a price tag of just $500.30 above the cost of a V-8 coupe, it was hard to pass up—and almost impossible to pass. By year's end, 10,773 Camaros rolled off the Norwood and Los Angeles assembly lines with the iron-headed "Rat" motor under their domed SS hoods.

RPO L89 differed little from the L78 in most

The Camaro's 396-ci engines were dressed up in chrome valve covers and a chrome, open-element air cleaner assembly. The 325-horsepower (shown) and 350-horsepower 396s featured a cast-iron intake manifold painted orange to match the block and heads. L78 396s were equipped with a natural-finish cast-aluminum intake manifold. The L89 396 used the same intake as the L78, plus natural-finish cast-aluminum cylinder heads.

respects. The "bottom end" was identical—the same pistons, crank, rods, four-bolt-main block, and cam. The "top end" was the same, too, with one critical difference: the cylinder heads were made of aluminum, not iron. Since the heads used the same design, port sizes, shapes, and so on, Chevy rated the L89 the same as the L78: 375 horsepower. But the lightweight aluminum heads shaved about 100 pounds off the front end, which had the same effect as adding power, plus it improved rise on acceleration and even helped improve handling while cornering (though the engine was still pretty hefty, compared to a small-block). Add to those benefits the fact that aluminum dissipates heat more quickly, and it was obvious to any racer that the L89 could be tweaked and tuned to deliver a fair bit more power than the L78. More aggressive timing curves and cam timing were possible, as was increased compression. But at $868.95, RPO L89 was hardly inexpensive. And with the same power rating as the L78 (which was nearly $400 cheaper), a mere 272 buyers anted up for the exotic L89.

COPO 427 1968 Camaros are still questionable, but the evidence that has been collected thus far indicates that at least some of Yenko's Super Camaros indeed may have been assembled with their 427-ci Mark IV engine right on Chevy's own assembly lines. At least one 1968 Yenko in existence has what appears to be a "numbers-matching" iron-headed version of the Corvette L88 engine under its fiberglass Yenko hood; the engine matches both the VIN and the Protect-O-Plate, and is properly coded "MV," matching Tonawanda engine assembly plant records for a special 427.

The only evidence of how to purchase the option was to place a COPO request for the #9737 Sports Car Conversion, which later in 1969 was Yenko's (and other "tuner" dealers') method of custom ordering their Camaros with a 140-mile-per-hour speedometer, special suspension changes, and other equipment. But in 1968, COPO 9737 could very well have been the covert code for a package that included the 427, which in 1969 had to be ordered separately (under COPO 9560 or 9561, depending on the desired 427). No one at or from GM seems to know for sure, nor do any dealers from the time.

Transmissions

Two new transmissions—RPOs MB1 and M22—were added to the Camaro option sheet in 1968, bringing the total transmission choices to eight: five manuals, two automatics, and a semiautomatic (essentially a PowerGlide automatic that drivers had to shift manually).

Manual Transmissions

The base transmission remained a three-speed manual gearbox. Available for six-cylinder and 327-ci V-8 engines, there wasn't much about the

Chevy's marketing name for the big-block V-8s was "TurboJet" (small-blocks, including the 327 and 350, were "Turbo-Fire" engines). This engine is the base L35 325-horsepower 396, which was still plenty impressive and featured a large spread–bore Rochester QuadraJet carburetor topped by an open-element air cleaner with a chrome-plated lid.

base three-speed to get excited about. Its cast-iron case was heavy, and its gear spread made it well suited to casual, economical, around-town driving, but little else.

As was the case the year before, RPO M13 netted a buyer a heavy-duty three-speed manual gearbox, provided they weren't ordering a six-cylinder or the Z28, L78, or L89 V-8 engines. With different first and second gear ratios plus straighter-cut cogs for all gears, the $79 option was a sound economical choice.

Moving up to a four-speed manual gearbox was a big financial jump. The cheapest four-speeds—the wide-ratio M20 and the close-ratio M21, both of which were built by GM's Muncie Gear division—were still $184.35. Both transmissions were essentially unchanged from 1967.

New to the manual transmission lineup was the M22 close-ratio Muncie four-speed. Outwardly similar to both the M20 and M21, the M22 featured nearly straight-cut gears that were significantly stronger than those in the M21, which had the same gear ratios. The straighter-cuts also gave

the M22 gearboxes a peculiar sound that was somewhat similar to a bunch of rocks being ground up in a blender; hence, the transmission earned the nickname "Rock Crusher." The M22 was only available in conjunction with RPOs Z28, L78, or L89, and only for those willing to part with $310.70, which a scant 1,277 buyers were.

Automatic Transmissions
The M35 two-speed PowerGlide and M40 three-speed Turbo-Hydra-Matic automatics stuck around on the option sheet basically unchanged from 1967, and with the same basic restrictions on which models and engines they were available with.

Semiautomatic Transmissions
RPO MB1 offered buyers the chance to experience an unusual transmission: the "Torque-Drive" semiautomatic. Like a manual gearbox, drivers had to shift gears on their own. But like an automatic, there was no clutch—a driver simply grabbed the shifter and pushed it forward

Ultimate big-block performance came in the form of the L78 396 with its 375 horsepower. The L78 was actually quite different from lesser 396s. Some of the components that differ include the following: cylinder block, heads, intake, crankshaft, connecting rods, pistons, camshaft, carburetor, and more!

Shown here is another view of the L78 396. The L78 was typically equipped with chrome dress-up items such as a chrome, open-element air cleaner and chrome valve covers.

Camaro windshield wiper motors were mounted to the firewall, and the actuator protruded through an opening into the cowl plenum, where the wiper arm linkage connected to it. The motor itself featured a 60 percent gloss-black finish, while the firewall itself was painted a flatter, 30 percent gloss black.

or pulled it backward. Unfortunately, the unit was based on the PowerGlide, so it had only two forward speeds, plus it was only available with six-cylinder models.

Driveshafts

All Camaros utilized tubular steel driveshafts with forged-steel input and output yokes. Depending on the assembly plant, shift, and time of year, some driveshafts were painted semiflat black, while others were left natural. It's also common for the driveshafts to feature small, brightly colored paint marks that indicated the application for which that driveshaft was intended; the marks allowed for quick identification on the assembly line, as driveshafts differed in length and yoke configura-

tion depending on the transmission and rear axle assembly in a particular vehicle.

Rear Axle Assemblies

Camaros continued to be equipped with either of two basic rear axle assemblies in 1968: the "10-bolt" assembly for most applications, and a heavy-duty "12-bolt" assembly for high-performance applications.

G80 became the RPO code for GM's Positraction limited-slip differential (formerly C80) and remained available with either differential assembly. Buyers could also select from a variety of gear ratios from a highway-friendly 2.56:1 to a drag strip–dominating 4.56:1, depending on their engine and transmission selections. Amazingly, optional rear axle ratios added just $2.15 to an order. Both assemblies were available with a variety of gear ratios (dependent upon engine and transmission combinations).

Unlike 1967, however, all 1968 Camaro rear axle assemblies featured a staggered shock arrangement, intended to minimize axle windup on hard acceleration. Unfortunately, the change also eliminated the factory-installed torque arm that had been installed on performance models in 1967.

As in 1967, the axle housing and associated parts were painted semigloss black.

Chassis

The same "semi-unitized" chassis construction served as the foundation of the 1968 Camaro as in 1967. The unitized passenger compartment was economical and reasonably strong, while the bolt-on front subframe assembly softened the ride and provided manufacturing flexibility. Unfortunately, performance models—particularly the high-torque 396s—proved capable of twisting and warping the body structure if subjected to aggressive driving on a regular basis.

Body Structure

The passenger compartment and trunk area were built as a unibody assembly of sheet metal and pinch-welds. This method was lightweight, reasonably strong, and inexpensive. Unfortunately, the unibody assembly results in fairly poor noise, vibration, and harshness characteristics since the suspension system and a number of other components are directly attached to the body structure.

The Camaro body structure is prone to rust in the typical spots: rocker panels, the bottom of the quarter panels, the trunk floor, and around the rear window. Because the body structure is responsible for the structural integrity of the vehicle, rust is more of a problem on the Camaro than on a more conventionally built car such as the Chevelle, which uses a body-on-frame design.

Subframe Assembly

The front portion of the chassis is comprised of a heavy-gauge steel subframe assembly that attaches to the unibody body structure with six rubber body mounts and heavy-duty bolts. The subframe serves as the mounting structure for the front suspension and steering components, as well as the engine and transmission.

The front wheels typically produce the harshest jolts and vibrations to the passenger compartment, but with the Camaro subframe's rubber mounts, those harsh signals are dampened, which gives the Camaro the solid feel of a much larger car.

In addition, because of the subframe's heavy-gauge steel construction, it's an exceptionally strong structure to which the front suspension can be connected. A sturdy structure is essential for accurate suspension action. By contrast, the Mustang's weaker, fully unitized body construction flexes and twists when subjected to suspension forces.

Floor Pan

The Camaro floor pan is an integral part of the body structure. The floor pans are typical formed sheet-metal construction and are welded and sealed to the body structure. The floor pans contain several drain holes that are plugged with removable sheet-metal discs. During the early production process, the body structure is submerged in a chemical bath to clean it and prepare it to receive primer and paint. The drain holes allow the chemicals to drain more completely from the body assembly. The drain plugs are installed with a sealant after the assembly is thoroughly dry.

Camaro floor pans generally exhibit only minor rust or corrosion unless subjected to severe conditions or neglect. Leaking door and window seals or convertible tops allow water to enter the passenger compartment and puddle up in the footwells, leading to rust formation, which can become quite severe if not treated early.

The convertible-only floor pan reinforcement plate continued to be used in 1968.

Wheels and Tires

A variety of wheels and tires continued to be available on the Camaro to enhance both its appearance and its performance. All wheels were of stamped-steel construction, in varying designs and sizes.

A number of different tire suppliers were used throughout the 1968 model year. In addition, the tires installed often varied between the two Camaro assembly plants in Norwood, Ohio, and Los Angeles, California.

Wheels

Two wheel designs were again available on 1968 Camaros: the basic steel wheel with any of several full wheel covers, and the RPO ZJ7 "Rally"-styled steel wheel, which featured a bright center cap and trim ring. The wheels were available in different diameters and widths, depending on the options ordered. The base wheel measured 14.0x5.5 inches. The SS options included Rally wheels that measured 14.0x6.0 inches. The Z28 received a 15.0x6.0-inch version of the Rally wheel. For 1968, the Rally wheel's center cap was updated with a "turbine"-style appearance.

Tires

A number of different tire makes, models, styles, and sizes were installed on Camaros at the two factories throughout the model year.

The majority of the tires were 7.35x14.0, including the base tires and RPO P58 whitewall tires. RPO PW7 put F70x14 two-ply white-stripe tires on a buyer's Camaro; PW8 was the code for F70x14 red-stripe tires, and PY4 and PY5 were fiberglass-belted versions of those respective tires. Z28s rolled away on E70x15 nylon tires.

Common makes and models were Goodyear Polyglas-GT and Firestone Wide-Oval for the performance tires; Uniroyal Tiger Paws were also common.

Suspension

Changes to the Camaro suspension system were few but significant in 1968. Spring and shock rates

This 1968 model shows off the stylish full wheel cover (left) with its mag-wheel appearance. Interestingly enough, the wheel covers were more expensive ($73.75, for RPO N96) than the cost of actual Rally Wheels ($31.60, for RPO ZJ7). The Butternut Yellow (code YY) SS features the minimalist-yet-stylish "dog dish" partial wheel covers (below left) on body-color steel wheels, with red-striped tires.

were revised to enhance ride and handling, but the big news was the replacement of the rear "Monoleaf" springs on all but the lowest-performance models with multileaf spring packs for better control and resistance to axle windup and wheel hop.

Front Suspension

The front suspension design was unchanged from 1967: unequal-length upper (short) and lower (long) A-arms. Both arms were painted semigloss black, though the ball joint end of the lower arm remained bare (due to the method of suspending the arm during painting). The spindle assembly, which connects to both the upper and lower ball joints, was either a natural cast-iron finish or painted semigloss black, as were the steering knuckles.

A hollow, tubular steel anti-roll bar continued to be used up front. Again, bars were either natural-finished steel or painted semigloss black. The mounting brackets were natural or semigloss black steel, and the end-links continued to be zinc-plated hardware.

Rear Suspension

Replacing 1967's single-leaf rear springs with multileaf spring packs was a seemingly simple but fundamental change to the 1968 Camaro. It provided immediate improvements in handling and acceleration, plus more easily allowed for variable spring rates, so the ride could be smoother without hampering performance potential. Note, however, that six-cylinder models and the 210- and 275-horsepower 327 models continued to rely on the Monoleaf springs. As in 1967, the leaf springs were either a natural steel finish or semigloss black.

Equally important was the change to a staggered rear shock arrangement, for which the left shock's lower mounting point was moved rearward of the axle centerline, while the right shock's lower mount remained ahead of the axle centerline. Staggering the shocks helped minimize wheel hop by controlling axle windup on hard acceleration. As the axle housing attempts to rotate (due to the tires' resistance against the ground), it will attempt to compress the forward shock, while simultaneously attempting to extend the rearward shock. The shock absorbers were painted semigloss gray.

Rear anti-roll bars were, again, noticeably absent from 1968 Camaros.

Brakes

While base Camaro brake systems were hardly cutting edge with their four-wheel drum assemblies, several options were available that greatly enhanced a Camaro's ability to shed speed.

The primary brake system was a typical hydraulic system with a dual-reservoir master cylinder and available power assist and front disc brake configuration. The cast-iron master cylinder featured a natural finish, as did the steel brake lines.

Again, the secondary brake system utilized natural-finish steel-stranded cables operated by the parking brake pedal to engage the rear brakes. The brake cables were encased in a spiral steel sheath from the firewall to a point beneath the driver's floor pan, where the single cable pulls a bracket to which each of the rear brake cables connects. The rear cables have a sheath that runs from the backing plate to a bracket on the rear subframe rail.

Front and Rear Drum Brakes

Four-wheel drum brakes were again standard on 1968 Camaros. The drums had a semigloss black finish, as did the steel backing plates. Wheel cylinders were also semigloss black.

RPO J50 added a vacuum-operated power assist to the drum brake system to reduce the brake pedal effort necessary to operate the brake system. The booster unit is a circular steel vacuum diaphragm assembly mounted between the master cylinder and the firewall. Power brake–equipped Camaros utilize different master cylinders from those without power brakes. In addition, the brake pedal assembly uses a different hinge point than non–power brake systems.

Front Disc/Rear Drum Brakes

Replacing the front drum brakes with available disc brakes provided a significant improvement in braking ability. RPO J52 not only rewarded shrewd buyers with the front disc assemblies, but also a power assist system, similar to RPO J50, although with a different master cylinder and different proportioning valve. The calipers and rotors were essentially the same as 1967 equipment.

Steering

Camaro steering systems are not unlike those of other Chevrolet models. Steering inputs are transferred from the steering wheel through a steering column to a recirculating-ball steering box, which converts the rotary motion into a linear motion that acts upon a series of linkages to ultimately steer the front wheels.

The steering wheels are large by today's standards: 16 inches in diameter for the standard wheel, and a similar size for the RPO N30 Deluxe wheel and the RPO N34 wood-grained wheel. The large wheel increased the driver's leverage, which reduced steering effort, but also reduced steering feel somewhat.

Steering wheel inputs traveled forward through either of two steering columns that were available: the standard, fixed-angle column or the RPO N33 tilt column. Both columns featured a chromed turn signal stalk with a round plastic knob on the left side of the column. Tilt-columns featured a shorter but similar-looking stalk forward of the turn signal lever to operate the tilt mechanism. Vehicles not equipped with a floor shifter featured a long chrome shift lever on the right side of the column. Both steering columns also featured a small hazard lamp switch on the right side of the column.

The steering column connects to a simple, semi-flat black-finish steel steering shaft, which in turn connects to the steering box through a flexible steering coupler, more commonly known as a "rag joint."

There were several different steering boxes available, each of which mounted to the left subframe rail between the front cross-member and the firewall, and featured a natural cast-iron finish with a natural-finished aluminum access cover. Standard was a non-assisted manual unit with a 24:1 gear ratio and linkage that resulted in a 28.3:1 overall ratio. RPO N44 quick-ratio steering yielded a 21.4:1 overall ratio, while Z/28s with RPO N44 provided a much lower 17.9:1 overall ratio for a far better feel and at-speed action.

Ordering RPO N40 provided a variable-ratio, engine-driven, hydraulic power steering assist. Without RPO N44, RPO N40 featured a 16.1:1 ratio on-center (15.5:1 overall) that reduced to a 12.4:1 ratio at full-lock. The same steering box was used for cars equipped with both RPOs N40 and N44, but differences in the steering linkage resulted in a higher-effort 14.3:1 overall ratio on-center.

A natural-finish cast-iron pitman arm connects the steering box output shaft to the parallel relay rod (more commonly called a "drag link" or "center link"), which is supported at the right subframe rail by the idler arm. The ends of the relay rod connect to inner tie-rod ends. Tie-rod adjustment sleeves connect the inner tie-rod ends to the outer tie-rod ends, which connect to the steering knuckles. The relay rod, idler arm, tie-rod ends, and steering knuckles were all natural-finished cast iron, while the tie-rod adjustment sleeves were natural-finished steel.

Fuel System

Nineteen sixty-eight Camaro fuel systems were largely unchanged from 1967 systems. The new engines used the same or similar equipment to carried-over engines. The L34 utilized the same cast-iron intake of the L35, and the same Rochester QuadraJet four-barrel carburetor. The L89, likewise, used the same intake and carburetor as the L78.

As with the intakes and carburetors, the 1968 assortment of fuel pumps, fuel lines, fuel tanks, fuel filters, and other related fuel system components were essentially unchanged from their 1967 equivalents.

Exhaust System

Camaro exhaust systems were simple and largely typical for the day: natural-finish (with some overspray near the cylinder heads) cast-iron exhaust manifolds collected gases from the engine, and then funneled them to individual "header" pipes. For single-exhaust systems, the left-hand header pipe crossed between the subframe cross-member and the oil pan sump to merge with the right-hand pipe to feed the intermediate pipe. The intermediate pipe ran rearward inside the transmission tunnel, then swept up and over the left-hand side of the rear axle assembly and into a single transverse-mounted muffler. A single tailpipe exited the right-hand side of the muffler, curved rearward, and dumped the exhaust gases out beneath the rear lower valance panel.

A dual-exhaust system, such as RPO N10, was similar, however, the individual header pipes did not merge, and the system utilized two individual intermediate pipes. RPO N10 still relied upon a single, transverse-mounted muffler, though with two inlets (one per side) and two outlets (again, one per side). The N10 tailpipes each curved rearward and exited beneath the valance panel, one on each side of the muffler.

RPO NF2 was a new option for 1968. As with N10, it was a dual-exhaust system, but the main difference was the use of a "deep-tone" transverse muffler, instead of the standard muffler. The result was a throatier, tougher rumble. RPO NF2 was standard with the Z28 and optional on most other V-8 Camaro models.

Again, all exhaust pipes and mufflers were natural-finished mild steel and were quite prone to rusting. Header and intermediate pipe diameters remained conservative: single-exhaust and small-block (except Z/28) dual-exhaust systems were comprised of pipes that measured 2.0 inches, while Z/28 and 396 dual-exhaust systems utilized 2.25-inch pipes for increased flow capacity and efficiency. Tailpipes measured 2 inches in diameter, regardless of the system.

The Z28 option-in-an-option tubular steel exhaust headers were again available, but were still shipped in the trunk, for the owner or dealer to install.

Cooling System

Virtually nothing changed about the Camaro cooling systems in 1968, which was just fine, since the 1967 systems had proven themselves reliable and effective.

A 50/50 mixture of ethylene glycol coolant and water circulates through the engine to absorb heat, then flows through the rubber upper radiator hose to the radiator, where it dissipates its heat to the air flowing through the radiator fins. The coolant then is drawn through the spring-reinforced (to prevent collapsing) rubber lower radiator hose by and through the water pump, and then into the engine again.

It's interesting to note that Chevrolet records indicate that just over 500 Camaros were equipped with an unlisted option: an engine-block heater system, which helped prevent the coolant/antifreeze from freezing in extremely cold temperatures when the engine wasn't in operation.

Meanwhile, the Camaro's "Astro Ventilation" and RPO C60 air conditioning were designed to cool the passengers.

Engine Cooling System

The engine cooling system used the same components and combinations as in 1967. Radiators with two rows, three rows, and four rows of cooling tubes were used for the low-, medium-, and high-performance applications. RPO V01's heavy-duty radiator added the next radiator size up from a model's standard radiator, while most air-conditioned (RPO C60) cars were equipped with three-row radiators.

Again, depending on the radiator and other options, a partial or full fan shroud was installed to improve safety and cooling efficiency. Likewise, a number of fans were available, differing in blade count, material, and whether they featured a viscous fan clutch or not. All of these items were similar or identical to their 1967 counterparts.

Passenger Cooling System

The heating, ventilation, and air conditioning systems were also much as they were in 1967, though they benefited from new outlets near the sides of the instrument panel. As before, a number of heating and cooling options were available, from the RPO C50 rear window defroster to full heater/defroster deletes (which had to be manually written on the order form).

Chapter 3

1969 Camaro

Overview

When the 1969 Camaros hit show rooms in September 1968, enthusiasts were stunned: the new Camaro looked almost completely different, and yet was entirely recognizable as a Camaro.

Chevrolet stylists reworked the sporty 1967–1968 Camaro into a lower, wider, more muscular machine for 1969 through careful—and exceptionally well-executed—changes to a number of the Camaro's body panels, including

Nineteen sixty-nine was a high point in both style and substance for the Camaro. Stylewise, nearly every body panel was redesigned yet managed to retain an obvious evolutionary connection to its past. Substancewise, the Camaro performance improved in nearly every respect, thanks to upgrades to cars such as the Z28 and SS-396, plus the addition of all-out factory options including this ultraexotic ZL1 COPO Camaro.

the fenders, quarter panels, door skins, grille, tail-lamp panel, and both valances, front and rear. New hoods were designed, too, although the old ones still fit.

Every 1969 model, down to the base car such as this one, featured the new, muscular-looking sheet metal with squared-off wheel openings and sharp body character lines. The result of the new panels was a wider, longer, and lower-looking Camaro to which the public instantly took a liking.

The changes were more than just skin-deep, though. A new instrument panel and other refinements to the interior made it more comfortable for long trips and short trips alike, while new and revised engines, plus a host of brake, suspension, and chassis updates enhanced performance and reliability.

Identification

Spotting a 1969 Camaro is a breeze for most Camaro enthusiasts.

The basic shape and appearance are similar to the 1967–1968 Camaros, but the front end, rear end, fenders, and quarter panels are quickly recognizable as 1969 equipment, as you'll soon understand (if you don't already).

First, the front end is quickly recognizable whether in Rally Sport (RS) trim or not. Non-RS 1969 Camaros have two large, round headlights (one per side) set into an argent silver bezel. The grille has a much more pronounced "V" to it, which results in the sides of the grille being quite recessed, giving the headlights a "bug-eyed" sort of appearance.

Rally Sport–equipped 1969 Camaros still utilized swing-away headlight doors, but the new doors were painted to match the body of the car and featured three horizontal "windows" that allowed light from the headlights to shine through in case the doors failed to open properly. The grille for RS cars had only a subtle "V" to it, and was oval in shape and black in color.

Unlike in years past, RS and non-RS 1969 Camaros used the same turn signal lamps, since they are located in the lower valance for both models. The two lamps are round (like 1967 models) and have the appearance of fog or driving lights. Some 1969 Camaros were also equipped with a unique new body-color front bumper, which really provided a clean appearance.

From the rear, it takes only a second to notice that the 1969 taillamps are wider than in 1967 and 1968, and have three segments arranged in a sawtooth appearance. The gas cap was relocated to behind the rear license plate (which was hinged to tilt down for access to the gas cap), but an emblem (which varied depending on options) continued to be positioned in the center of the taillamp panel. As in 1967 and 1968, non-RS models still incorporated the reverse-indicator lamps into the taillamps, but in those cases, the reverse-indicator lamp consisted of only a small, roughly 1.5-inch square of white translucent plastic set into the center of the middle lens segment. Also as in the past, RS

models usedrectangular reverse-indicator lamps mounted in the rear lower valance panel, beneath the rear bumper.

Nineteen sixty-nine Camaros are perhaps even more recognizable from the sides, thanks to the new fenders and quarter panels, which each feature squared-off wheel openings (compared to the round openings of 1967–1968). In addition, the 1969 panels feature attractive flarelike creases that sweep back off the tops of the wheel openings, giving the car an appearance of speed, even when at rest. The quarter panels also sport simulated vent louvers between the door opening and the front of the rear wheel opening (cars equipped with [Regular Production Option] RPOs Z21 or Z22 are equipped with bright trim for those vent louvers, accentuating the louvers).

Two new hoods also debuted in 1969: a redesigned Super Sport hood, which continued to utilize twin, simulated vent stacks; and the legendary "cowl induction" RPO ZL2 hood, which Chevrolet called the "Super Scoop" hood in its advertisements.

Super Sport models, such as the 396-powered model with Rally Sport equipment, were exceptional to look at and to drive. The 396 continued to be available in "hot," "hotter," and "hottest" variations: 325, 350, and 375 horsepower, respectively. New "hockey stick" striping on the front fenders and doors gave the SS an updated appearance.

For the second time in just three years, the Camaro was selected to pace the Indy 500, and Chevy again capitalized on the occasion by releasing limited-edition "Pace Car Replicas" in both coupe (RPO Z10) and convertible form (Z11) (above). The cars featured a Dover White body with Hugger Orange Z/28-style hood and deck lid stripes. Inside, the car sported a unique orange interior with orange-and-black houndstooth

fabric inserts on the seats. The power came from standard SS offerings. Shown below is a pace replica at speed on Michigan International Speedway. Note the bold lettering on the doors. The lettering decals were supplied in the trunk; buyers had the option of installing them or not. The official-looking racing flags on the back bumper of this replica were added by the owner, but they are a nice touch.

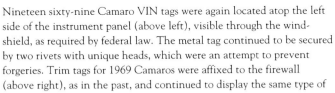

Nineteen sixty-nine Camaro VIN tags were again located atop the left side of the instrument panel (above left), visible through the windshield, as required by federal law. The metal tag continued to be secured by two rivets with unique heads, which were an attempt to prevent forgeries. Trim tags for 1969 Camaros were affixed to the firewall (above right), as in the past, and continued to display the same type of information: build date, model and body, paint, interior trim, and a few noteworthy options. Note that this tag is incorrectly painted body color; from the factory the tags were the same 30 percent gloss black as the firewall. This image (below) clearly shows the location of the trim tag, slightly above and to the right-hand side of the master cylinder and/or power brake booster.

Vehicle Identification Number (VIN)

The 1969 Camaro VIN tag continued to be mounted to the top of the instrument panel, visible through the left side of the windshield, as mandated by federal law. The tag featured the same design and characteristics as the 1968: flat-black-painted tin stamped from behind and riveted to the vehicle structure, forward of the dash pad.

For information on how to decode Camaro VIN tags, refer to Appendix B.

Trim Data Tag

Nineteen sixty-nine trim tags differed little from 1967–1968 versions, in terms of construction, placement, or coding. Still affixed to the upper left cowl (firewall) panel, inside the engine compartment, adjacent to the windshield wiper motor, the tag was coded to identify (for assembly-line workers) the appropriate body color and interior trim to apply to the car. In 1969, some additional information was also coded into the tag, including one of several possible exterior trim codes.

For information on how to decode Camaro trim tags, please refer to Appendix A.

Engine Stamping

As had become customary for Chevrolet (and all GM divisions), the engine block was coded with a stamp set to identify the engine model and the vehicle for which it was destined. For V-8 engines, the codes were stamped into a machined pad just in front of the right cylinder head (the machined surface was an extension of the right-side block

1969 CAMARO PRODUCTION FIGURES

RPO	Description	Units
12337	Camaro sport coupe (6-cyl)	53,523
12337	Camaro sport coupe (6-cyl)	34,541
12367	Camaro convertible (6-cyl)	1,707
12437	Camaro sport coupe (V-8)	190,971
12467	Camaro convertible (V-8)	15,866
L34	350-hp 396-ci V-8 (requires Z27)	2,018
L35	325-hp 396-ci V-8 (requires Z27)	6,752
L48	295-hp 350-ci V-8 (included with Z27)	22,339
L78	375-hp 396-ci V-8 (requires Z27)	4,889
L89	375-hp 396-ci V-8 w/alum. heads (req's Z27)	311
Z22	Rally Sport package	37,773
Z27	Super Sport package	34,932
Z28	Special Performance package	20,302

1969 CAMARO COLOR AND TRIM COMBINATIONS

Series	Trim	INTERIOR TRIM COLORS AND RPO CODES					
		Black	Dark Blue	Med. Red	Med. Green	Dark Green	Parchment
Standard Interior	Vinyl buckets	711	715	718	721	723	
Custom Interior	Vinyl buckets	712	716	719	722	725	730
(RPO Z87)	Cloth buckets, houndstooth	713					

EXTERIOR PAINT AND RPO CODES									
LOS	Nor	RPO	Color	Black	Dark Blue	Med. Red	Med. Green	Dark Green	Parchment
S O	X	10	Tuxedo Black	X	X	X	X	X	X
S O	S O	40	Butternut Yellow	X				X	X
X	X	50	Dover White	X	X	X	X	X	X
S O	X	51	Dusk Blue	X	X				X
X	X	52	Garnet Red	X		X			X
X	X	53	Glacier Blue	X	X				X
X	X	55	Azure Turquoise	X					X
X	X	57	Fathom Green	X			X	X	X
X	X	59	Frost Green	X	X		X	X	X
S O	X	61	Burnished Brown	X					X
X	S O	63	Champagne	X				X	X
X	X	65	Olympic Gold	X				X	X
S O	X	67	Burgundy Maroon	X		X			X
X	X	69	Cortez Silver	X	X	X		X	X
X	X	71	Le Mans Blue	X					X
X	X	72	Hugger Orange	X					X
X	X	76	Daytona Yellow	X					X
X	X	79	Rallye Green	X					X
S O	X	51-53	Dusk Blue/Glacier Blue	X	X				X
X	X	53-50	Glacier Blue/Dover White	X	X				X
S O	X	53-51	Glacier Blue/Dusk Blue	X	X				X
X	X	55-50	Azure Turq./Dover White	X					X
S O	S O	61-63	Burn. Brown/Champagne	X					X
X	X	65-50	Olympic Gold/Dover White	X				X	X

L indicates Los Angeles-built cars; N indicates Norwood-built cars. SO indicates available by Special Order only. Convertible models not available with two-tone paint schemes.

The standard Camaro hood for 1969 models is, again, mostly flat and featureless, except for the lengthwise character crease.

deck surface); six-cylinder models were stamped at the front of the engine adjacent to the head, as well.

Body

In 1969, the Camaro once again looked like nothing else on the road. The new, aggressive looks of the 1969 models really helped draw people into dealerships and were often a large part of the reason why buyers selected the Camaro over a competitor.

Two body styles continued to be available: a coupe and a convertible, both of which shared nearly all of the same body panels, from the entire front clip (fenders, hood, header panel, valance, and cowl panel) to doors, deck lid, taillamp panel, and rear lower valance. Few 1969 panels were interchangeable with 1967–1968 models, mainly just the hood, deck lid, and roof.

Body Styles

The Camaro was again available in two body styles: a semifastback two-door coupe, and a similar-looking two-door convertible. Color palettes and combinations were again updated, and now included a number of exciting colors, including Daytona Yellow and Hugger Orange. Refer to the accompanying Color and Trim Combination chart for more information.

Hoods

Nineteen sixty-nine Camaros were equipped with one of three hood designs, and a fourth was available over the counter that year.

The first design is the base hood, which is largely flat and featureless, save for a lengthwise character ridge running down the center of the hood, front to back.

The second hood is the Super Sport (SS) hood, which, as in 1967 and 1968, uses two simulated vent stacks. However, the 1969 hood does not feature the large raised section on which those grilles were mounted in previous years.

The third hood was the all-new "cowl induction" hood, available under RPO ZL2. Perhaps the most recognizable and most-copied hood design in history, the ZL2 hood—which Chevy called the "Super Scoop" in advertising at the time—featured a functional cold-air induction system at the rear of the hood, just ahead of the windshield cowl panel. The ZL2 hood was available with any SS or the Z28, and it was also standard equipment on both the 9560 (ZL1) and 9561 (L72) Central Office Production Order (COPO) cars.

The fourth hood, which was only available over the counter from a GM parts dealer, was a fiberglass version of the ZL2 "cowl induction" hood. The only reason this is significant and worth mentioning is that for many years it was believed that the fiberglass hood was installed on the assembly line, but so-called "numbers matching" cars should always have a steel hood.

Grille Assemblies

As part of the 1969 Camaro's restyling, the grille was redesigned with its most pronounced "V" shape to date. The base grille was argent silver, as were the matching headlamp surrounds. The Z28 and Super Sport models received a more ominous black grille, as did any 1969 Camaro equipped with Rally Sport equipment.

The Rally Sport grille, however, was narrower than the base grille, and the headlamp doors and surrounding trim were body color.

Front Bumper

The front bumper of the 1969 Camaro had to be redesigned to match and complement the new fenders and grille.

In addition to the standard chromed steel front bumper, a new code was added to the option list: the RPO VE3 "body color" front bumper. The VE3 bumper had a steel core to help hold the bumper's shape, but it featured a unique rubber-like substance that Chevy Called "Endura" or "Endura Flex."

Once again, RPO V31 bumper guards were an option for all 1969 Camaros except those with Endura bumpers.

1969 Camaro Accent Striping Color Availability for RPOs, D90, D96, and DX1

Body Color	Sport Coupe Vinyl Roof Color						Convertible Coupe Top Color	
	(None)	Black	Parchment	Dark Brown	Dark Blue	Midnight Green	Black	White
Tuxedo Black	White	White	White			White	White	White
Butternut Yellow	Black	Black	Black	Black			Black	Black
Dover White	Black	Black	Black		Black	Black	Black	Black
Dusk Blue	White	White	White		White		White	White
Garnet Red	Black*	Black*	White†				Black*	White†
Glacier Blue	Black	Black	White		Black		Black	White
Azure Turquoise	Black	Black	White				Black	White
Fathom Green	White	White	White			White	White	White
Frost Green	Black	Black	White			Black	Black	White
Burnished Brown	White	White	White	White			White	White
Champagne	Black	Black	White	Black			Black	White
Olympic Gold	Black	Black	White	Black			Black	White
Burgundy Maroon	Red	Red	White				Red	White
Cortez Silver	Black	Black	White		Black		Black	White
Le Mans Blue	Black	Black	White				Black	White
Hugger Orange	White	Black	White				Black	White
Daytona Yellow	Black	Black	Black				Black	Black
Rallye Green	White	Black	White				Black	White
Dusk Blue/Glacier Blue	White							
Glacier Blue/Dover White	White							
Glacier Blue/Dusk Blue	Black							
Azure Turq./Dover White	White							
Burn. Brown/Champagne	White							
Olympic Gold/Dover White	White							

*Red with Black interior. †Red with Red interior.

The SS hood was similar to the 1967–1968 SS hood, with their simulated vents. As in 1968, only one style of vent is used on 1969 hoods, regardless of whether a given SS featured a 350 or 396 engine: each vent insert panel features four square simulated vent "stacks".

Rear Bumper
The 1969 rear bumper design was unique to the year, due to changes in vehicle width and quarter panel design. Unlike the front end, however, the rear bumper continued to be available only in chrome-plated steel.

Bumper guards were available as RPO V32, but were included on Z28 models.

Sides
The Camaro's profile is comprised of several body panels, primarily the fender, door, quarter panel, and roof. Of these, only the fender and quarter panel changed from previous years (which were largely the same as each other).

For 1969, the profile retained a familiar look to that of earlier Camaros, but thanks to its squared-off wheelwells and fender and quarter panel sculpting, the car took on a longer, lower, wider appearance—more so than the actual dimensional changes were responsible for.

Again, various options added bright trim moldings to the wheel openings, the rocker panels, and elsewhere. RPO Z21 added bright trim to the wheel openings and roof drip rails (except for convertibles, which don't have drip rails), plus simulated louvers on the rear quarter panels and bright bezels for the headlamp and taillamp assemblies. From the side, RPO Z22 cars were virtually indistinguishable from the Z21 cars except for the "rally sport" nameplates on the fenders (and don't forget that the Z22s also had the hidden headlamps and blacked-out grille).

A number of options, including RPOs DX1, D90, D86, and Z27 (Super Sport), added striping to the sides of the cars, from thin pinstripes following

Perhaps the most famous hood design to come out of the 1960s is the legendary "cowl induction" hood (above), officially known as the RPO ZL2 special ducted hood, which Chevy called the "Super Scoop" hood in its advertising. The ZL2 hood (right) earned its "cowl induction" nickname because its rear-facing opening overhangs the cowl vents, allowing the hood to draw cool outside air from the base of the windshield.

Viewed from the side, the ZL2 hood was clean and simple, the center rising roughly 2 inches above the rest of the hood. The sides of the scoop also gave stylists an ideal spot for engine-displacement emblems; those emblems were deleted, however, on most 427-powered "COPO" Camaros.

The front end of the 1969 Camaro resembled its predecessors, but had a more sharply angled "V"-shaped grille, which resulted in the headlights having more pronounced surrounds.

As part of the redesign for 1969, the standard grille was given a more noticeable "V" shape, plus a larger, rectangular grille pattern. Grilles for base cars and Z/28s feature a grayish/silver finish. Super Sport models feature a blacked-out grille.

the fender character lines to partial striping that existed primarily on the hood, but flowed down the fenders, similar to the "bumblebee stripe" of old. The SS stripe, included with RPO Z27, was again changed for 1969; with a vertical portion that runs up the front of the fender, then turns and runs rearward along the fender and door, the stripe bears a striking resemblance to a hockey stick and is often referred to as such.

Another new change for 1969 was the availability of two-tone paint treatments, which typically consisted of one color for the bulk of the body, and a different color for the rocker area. See the Color and Trim Combinations chart in this chapter.

Roof

Three types of roofs remained available on 1969 Camaros: painted steel, vinyl-covered steel, and convertible.

While 1967 and 1968 painted steel roofs were always body color from the factory, with the addition of two-tone paint treatments the roof could just as easily be a complementary or contrasting color to the rest of the body, resembling a vinyl roof, but without the vinyl.

Again, vinyl roof covers were glued to a semi-finished steel roof, but the 1969 vinyl roof featured an attractive new look. Rather than being full width, as in the past, running from drip rail to drip rail, the 1969 vinyl roof ended just a few

Since the ends of the grille were more recessed than in the past, that left more of the headlights exposed. Deep headlight surrounds tastefully hid the headlamp buckets. As in 1967, the 1969 Camaro again featured round turn signal/parking lamps. Since the lamps were mounted in the lower valance panel, they were the same for both non-RS and RS cars alike. As mentioned previously, RS grilles had a smaller, oval look to them, which emphasized the new body-colored headlamp doors. Unlike the standard grille, RS grilles were nearly flat, with only a subtle "V" shape, when viewed from above (below). RS grilles are black in color.

The "Endura" VE3 body-colored bumper was also available with the standard (non-RS) front end, as this Z/28 clearly shows.

All 1969 Camaros featured subtle, simulated vents (far left) stamped into the quarter panel sheet metal between the door opening and the rear wheel opening. On models equipped with the RPO Z21 Style Trim option, bright trim accentuated these simulated vents. The RPO Z21 simulated vent louver trim (left) was chrome plated with black accents and secured to the quarter panel with sheet-metal speed nuts from inside the panel.

inches shy of the drip rail on each side, terminating beneath a piece of bright metal trim. Due to the redesign, vinyl material was not applied to the A-pillars, so the 1969 tops consisted of just four pieces: the roof center section, two side pieces, and a piece for the deck lid filler panel. Vinyl roofs were available in black or off-white to match or contrast with the vehicle's paint color.

Convertible top color choices shrank to just two: black or white (parchment). The top material remained a canvaslike fabric with a sewn-in clear vinyl rear window. The top's framework was primarily steel, and was available in either manual or power-operated configurations. The forward edge of the roof was secured by two latches to an oversized windshield header trimmed in bright

1969 CAMARO MONTHLY PRODUCTION

	Los Angeles		Norwood	
1969 Models				
Month	**Start**	**End**	**Start**	**End**
August (08)	500001	500999	500001	502000
September (09)	501000	502310	502001	512133
October (10)	502311	506631	512134	530337
November (11)	506632	510583	530338	551862
December (12)	510584	513816	561863	569987
January (01)	513817	520247	569988	589720
February (02)	520248	525388	589721	607164
March (03)	525389	528108	607165	623587
April (04)	528109	530155	623588	637106
May (05)	530156	531026	637107	650323
June (06)	531027	531163	650324	664008
July (07)			664009	669119
August* (08)			669120	678253
September* (09)			678254	692607
October* (10)			692608	707932
November* (11)			707933	711922

*1969 Model Year only. Figures courtesy of the United States Camaro Club (Note: Monthly start/end units are approximate). Production run extended due to a union strike that delayed the launch of the 1970 models.

metal. Where the top met the body panels on the sides and rear of the car, bright metal trim secured the fabric to the body.

Glass/Windows

Libby Owens Ford continued to be Chevrolet's source for Camaro windows in 1969. The windows are marked "LOF" and "Safety Flo-Lite" and feature date-coding to make identification of original windows possible.

Tinted windows were available under RPO A01 (all windows) and A02 (windshield only). Electrically operated power side windows were available under RPO A31.

The windshield is laminated safety glass, which breaks on impact but does not shatter.

The side and rear windows are safety plate glass, which shatters on impact.

Nineteen sixty-nine models again used a rectangular outside rearview mirror.

The windshield and rear window are secured to the vehicle with a ropelike bead of black adhesive. Bright metal trim attaches to anchors secured to the window channel and fills the gap between the glass and the window channel, covering the trim and minimizing the amount of debris that can enter the window channel and cause water drainage problems.

A rear window defroster was available via RPO C50 and consisted of a blower motor that mounted to the underside of the rear package shelf and utilized a grille that mounted to the top of the shelf. When activated by the switch on the instrument panel, the motor circulated warm air from within the passenger compartment against the rear window.

Mirrors

For 1969, the outside rearview mirror remained rectangular in shape, and the inside rearview mirror was virtually unchanged from the year before.

Option D33, the remote-control left-hand outside rearview mirror, was carried over from 1968.

A third mirror was available in 1969: option D34, the visor vanity mirror.

Headlamps

As before, 1969 Camaros featured two large, round, sealed-beam headlamp units; one lamp was mounted to each side of the grille. The 1969 headlamps were moved inward several inches, away from the sides of the grille. Original-equipment lamp units were supplied by Guide and are identifiable by a triangle shape cast into the center of the lens with "T-3" in its center.

Unless Rally Sport equipment (RPO Z22) was ordered, the headlamp units were exposed at all times, and were surrounded by a metal bezel, which was itself inside an argent silver plastic headlamp surround.

For the second year in a row, the RPO Z22 hidden-headlamp system was redesigned. The change in 1968 to vacuum-operated doors had greatly improved reliability over the electric-powered doors of 1967. The changes for 1969 were purely for aesthetics.

Instead of the solid black plastic doors of 1967 and 1968, the 1969 headlamp doors now featured three metal grilles through body-color doors. Not only was the new look dramatically different and far more attractive, but the slots in the doors allowed some light to shine through even in the event the system malfunctioned, preventing the doors from opening.

Nineteen sixty-nine also featured a unique headlamp washer system that was included with RPO Z22 and available separately as RPO CE1. The system, which was comprised of two small sprayer nozzles plus hoses that drew fluid from the

The Rally Sport front end was dramatically different in 1969 with body-color headlamp doors that contrasted nicely with the blacked-out, flat oval grille. The body-color headlamp doors and surrounds gave a unified look to the front end and resulted in what many enthusiasts consider to be a much more pleasing, integrated look than previous RS designs. In addition to matching the body better, the new headlamp doors featured three small, rectangular metal grilles (below) that allowed light to shine through in the event the vacuum-operated door mechanism failed to function properly. Also note the headlamp washer nozzle (mounted to the underside of the header panel), the round turn signal lamp, and this car's RPO VE3 body-colored front bumper, which was actually made of a composite rubber that resisted dents and never rusts.

windshield washer reservoir, cost just $15.80, yet only 116 buyers (in addition to the 36,773 RS buyers) benefited from it.

Taillamps

Again, part of the 1969 redesign was a new, wider taillamp panel, which featured wider, lower taillamps. The new taillamp assemblies featured three segments arranged in a sawtooth fashion. A chrome-plated bezel trimmed the taillamps, and on cars equipped with RPO Z21, the taillamps were bisected horizontally, which gave the appearance of six taillamp segments.

Rally Sport cars continued to have their back-up lamps mounted beneath the rear bumper, in the lower valance panel, while non-RS cars devoted a small portion of their middle taillamp segments to the white translucent back-up lamps.

Taillamp lenses were date-coded in 1969 and have a code identifying their intended use, and again the assemblies use only clear bulbs.

Turn Signals

Front turn signal indicator lamps reverted to a round shape from the rectangular shape of 1968, but thanks to the new RS design, the same valance-mounted lamps were used regardless of whether the car was equipped with RPO Z22 Rally Sport equipment or not.

The large, low-mounted turn signals actually gave the turn signal lamps the appearance of fog or driving lights, not unlike those used on night-driven racecars. Their placement—mounted just outboard of the center-mounted license plate—further nurtured the driving light image. As in the past, the lenses were clear plastic and the bulbs were amber or yellow.

Marker Lamps

The 1969 side marker lamps were redesigned and relocated higher on the fender. The short, wide lamps again accentuated the 1969 body's long, low, wide style. A chrome-plated plastic bezel was used, while the lenses were amber plastic for the front and red plastic in the rear.

Back-up Lamps

As in the past, non-RS back-up lamps were incor-

Another subtle styling cue used to differentiate SS models was the flat-black treatment given to the taillamp panel (except on black cars, which retained a body-color gloss-black panel). Note the taillamp configuration on this non-RS model.

As in the past, a number of taillamp panel identification emblems were used in 1969. One change for 1969, however, was that the emblems were no longer affixed to the gas cap, as the fuel filler neck had been relocated to behind the now-hinged rear license plate. Base cars received a large Chevy "bow tie" emblem, while RS models received this "RS" emblem.

porated into the standard taillamp assemblies, while RS cars had their back-up lamps mounted in the lower valance panel, beneath the rear bumper. In all cases, the backup lamp lenses relied on clear plastic and clear lamps.

Fuel Filler Cap

The fuel filler neck was relocated in 1969. Rather than exiting through the taillamp panel, the new neck was tucked neatly behind the flip-down license plate frame. The design change resulted in a cleaner rear-end appearance, without a large "wart" in between the taillamp assemblies. It also served a safety role, minimizing the chance of fire or explosion in a rear-end

collision, since the fuel tank was no longer rigidly attached to the body structure.

However, because the taillamp panel was prime "advertising" space, Chevy saw fit to equip Camaros with model identification in the former gas cap location—and thereby helped "break up" what would have been a massive expansive of unused space.

The actual emblems used changed somewhat from 1968, but the same rules of replacement applied: a blue Chevy bow tie was used for base cars (and COPOs). RS, SS, and Z/28 models each received their own appropriate emblems.

Deck Lid

As before, the 1969 deck lid was hardly a topic of conversation among enthusiasts. Were it not for the fact that the RPO D80 spoiler bolted to the deck lid, there would be little at all to mention about the deck lid panel itself.

The same deck lid panel was used regardless of body style or model. Like the 1968 models, the 1969s featured a script "Camaro" emblem with the words "BY CHEVROLET" carved into a small rectangular bar that underlined the Camaro emblem.

Deck Lid Spoiler

The RPO D80 front and rear spoilers that debuted in 1968 continued for early 1969 models, but by January 1970, the rear spoiler had been redesigned to be wider with a less severe angle. The new-style

In keeping with the longer, lower, wider styling theme of 1969, the taillamp assemblies grew. The new units, like this base assembly (right), were much wider and featured a sawtooth design (another styling theme of the year, used for items such as the auxiliary gauge cluster) with three "sections." All lenses were red (with clear bulbs) except the center section, which featured an inset translucent lens for the back-up lamps (which used clear bulbs, too). RPO Z21 Style Trim (below right) added bright metal trim around the taillamp assemblies, which also bisected the lens into upper and lower halves.

spoiler does not fit 1967—1968 Camaros, due to the new width. Each spoiler design required holes to be drilled through the deck lid, then it was a simple matter of inserting the spoiler's mounting studs through the holes and securing the assembly with sheet-metal speed nuts.

Again, on vehicles equipped with both Z/28-style stripes—which included RPOs Z10, Z11, and Z28—and D80 spoilers, the spoiler was installed prior to application of the stripes, so the area beneath the spoiler did not have striping paint.

The front spoiler continued on the same as in 1968.

Stripes and Bodyside Moldings

Striping options expanded again, in 1969, as they had done each year before. Stripe treatments were included with no less than nine options: DX1, D90, D96, Z10, Z11, Z21, Z22, Z27, and Z28.

Pinstripes, now referred to as "Fender Striping," were again applied to the sides of Camaros ordered with RPO Z21 Style Trim Group or RPO

The RS package added a number of nice changes to the rear of 1969 Camaros, including "remote" back-up lamps mounted beneath the bumper in the rear lower valance panel. Chrome bumperettes were another nice touch. Note that this Z/28's striping goes over the rear spoiler, but not beneath it, as was the proper configuration on cars equipped with spoilers and stripes from the factory.

No matter the model, the 1969 Camaro had a racy, aggressive appearance from any angle, as this base 307-powered car (above) shows. Note the lack of a rear deck lid spoiler. RPO D80 added a front air dam (right), beneath the lower valance panel, plus a rear spoiler atop the deck lid, as shown here. Two rear spoiler styles were used in 1969: some early models were equipped with the narrow (and lower) 1967–1968 version until supplies were used up, when production switched to the new, wider, and taller 1969 version.

Z22 Rally Sport equipment. For 1969, the stripe design had changed, however, and now only highlighted the character lines that swept off the tops of the fender and quarter panel wheel openings. The stripes were originally hand-applied.

Sport Striping, which listed as RPO D90 for $25.30 and was included as part of the RPO Z27 SS equipment, employed a bold "hockey stick" stripe along the fenders and doors.

Hood and Deck Lid Stripes had been a mainstay of RPO Z28's equipment list, but in 1969, the stripes were also available on the RPO Z10 and Z11 Indy 500 Pace Car replica options. The stripe dimensions were virtually identical to those of 1968, despite the body changes (remember, the hood, roof, and deck lid are essentially the same as in years passed).

Window Moldings consisted of bright metal trim surrounding the windshield and rear window of all 1969 Camaros.

Wheel Opening Moldings were installed on cars ordered with RPO Z21 or RPO Z22. The moldings were bright metal.

Roof Drip Rail Moldings were also part of

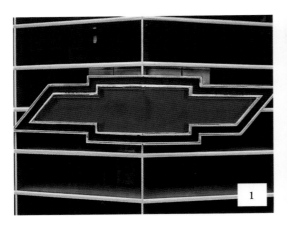

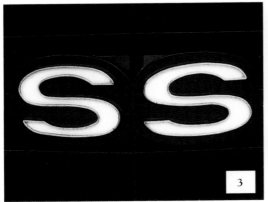

The standard grille emblem (1) is a blue "bow tie," mounted in the center of the grille. Cars equipped with RPO Z22 Rally Sport equipment received large, easy-to-read "RS" letters (2) as the center-mounted grille emblem. "SS" letters (3) were applied to the center of the grille of all 1969 Camaros equipped with RPO Z27 Super Sport equipment—even those equipped with Z22 Rally Sport equipment. RPO Z28 includes a special "Z/28" emblem (4), which was mounted toward the lower left-hand side (right side, when viewed from the front) of the grille. Though the option code was "Z28" (no slash), all emblems and Chevy literature and advertisements identified the car as a "Z/28". Chevy began identifying engine displacement with numeric emblems on the front of Camaro fenders (5) in 1968, and in 1969 the numbers were located next to a single, side marker lamp bezel. Note the redesigned marker lamps, which looked less like an afterthought, as the 1968 lamps had been often criticized. The Camaro 396 emblems (6) were a subtle warning sign to would-be competitors.

options RPO Z21 (Style Trim Group) and RPO Z22 (Rally Sport equipment). These bright metal moldings could be installed on any coupe but were not installed on convertible models, which have no drip rails.

Vinyl Roof Moldings were a bit more abundant in 1969, thanks to the new vinyl roof style that required lengths of trim to secure the sides of the vinyl roof, a few inches inward of the drip rails.

Door Edge Guards, RPO B93, were again an extremely popular and inexpensive way to protect the rear edge of the doors from scratches and paint chips that could result from the occasional bump against another car or a wall.

Emblems and Graphics

There was a truly dizzying array of emblems and graphics available on 1969 Camaro models, depending on the specific model and options ordered.

Header Panel and Deck Lid Emblems were the same style as in 1968—a large "Camaro" script with a small "Chevrolet" rectangle below. Again, on cars with factory-applied hood and deck lid (Z/28-style) stripes, the stripe was "knocked out" beneath the emblem, so the emblem was always installed against a body-color background. Stripes applied by dealers or independent painters typically did not feature this level of attention to detail.

While other Camaro models featured engine-displacement badges on the leading edge of the fenders, the Z/28 alone (7) featured a model-designation emblem: "Z/28". All Camaros in 1969—except Rally Sports—featured an emblem on the fenders (8), between the wheel opening and the door panel, which had the word "Camaro" written in script. Rally Sport models featured a block-lettered "Rally Sport" emblem, instead. Super Sport models (9) received the bold "SS" letters beneath the Camaro script emblem on the fenders. The block-lettered "Rally Sport" emblems (10) were a subtle but tasteful identity change for the upscale RS package.

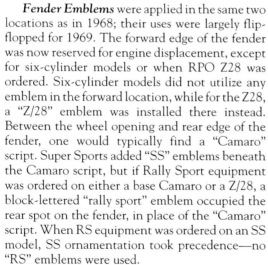

Fender Emblems were applied in the same two locations as in 1968; their uses were largely flip-flopped for 1969. The forward edge of the fender was now reserved for engine displacement, except for six-cylinder models or when RPO Z28 was ordered. Six-cylinder models did not utilize any emblem in the forward location, while for the Z28, a "Z/28" emblem was installed there instead. Between the wheel opening and rear edge of the fender, one would typically find a "Camaro" script. Super Sports added "SS" emblems beneath the Camaro script, but if Rally Sport equipment was ordered on either a base Camaro or a Z/28, a block-lettered "rally sport" emblem occupied the rear spot on the fender, in place of the "Camaro" script. When RS equipment was ordered on an SS model, SS ornamentation took precedence—no "RS" emblems were used.

Grille Emblems were used on all models, and were centered on the grille, except on the Z/28, which had its emblem mounted toward the lower left-hand corner of the grille. Base Camaro models used the blue Chevy bow tie. SS models used the "SS" letters, again, regardless of whether the engine was a 350 or 396 V-8. Rally Sport models used the "RS" emblem unless combined with the RPO Z22 SS equipment or RPO Z28, in which case emblems for those options took precedence.

Interior

As with the exterior, the 1969 Camaro interior received a redesign, focused primarily on the instrument panel.

A third trim level, RPO Z23 Special Interior, joined the base and RPO Z87 Custom Interiors (the latter of which actually included Z23). As in the past, the base interior was simple but attractive: all-vinyl bucket seats, vinyl-covered door panels with separate armrests, and simple emblems and controls. The Custom Interior was a modestly priced upgrade that rewarded buyers with molded door panels with integral armrests, more pleasing controls, upscale emblems, and high-styled seats. In between was the new Special Interior, which added a passenger grab bar, a wood-accented steering wheel, and bright medal trim to the base interior.

Instrument Panels

The new-for-1969 instrument panel was available in two configurations: with air conditioning and without it. Both designs featured two large square gauge pods, plus a smaller pod between them, above the steering column. The left pod held a round-faced 120-mile-per-hour speedometer on most models, although a 140-mile-per-hour unit was installed in performance models, such as the

Inside, the 1969 Camaro was as updated as the outside, featuring a new instrument panel, new seats, new door panels, and more. This is a Z11 Indy Pace Car Replica SS model with the unique orange-and-black houndstooth fabric seat inserts and the Custom Interior trim level.

As in the past, even the standard Camaro interior was a comfortable place to pass time, though somewhat sparse as this plainish black interior exhibits. Still, with bucket seats and four-speed shifter poking through the floor, what more could a performance nut want?

The Custom interior featured richer fabrics, more attractive molded door panels, and other changes that provided a wealthier appearance. This car features the optional black-and-white houndstooth fabric seat inserts, simulated wood trim on the instrument panel, a four-speed, floor console, and auxiliary gauges. Note that the steering wheel is incorrect.

The auxiliary gauges delivered to buyers who selected RPO U17 featured the same stepped, sawtooth-style design used in 1968. Unfortunately, the gauges were hardly legible and required the driver to take his (or her) eyes way off the road to look down near the floor. The four gauges are fuel level and oil pressure in the front, plus ammeter and water temperature in the rear.

Z/28 and COPO cars. The center pod was used for a clock, when ordered. The right pod was used for a fuel gauge and idiot lights, except when U16 (tachometer) was ordered, in which case U17 special instrumentation was required, in order to relocate the fuel gauge to the console-mounted gauge cluster.

At each end of the instrument panel are directional vertical, rectangular heating, ventilation, and air conditioning system vents. These replaced the round vents on 1968 Camaros.

The air conditioning version of the instrument panel contained slender, horizontal air conditioning vent outlets in the center of the instrument panel, mounted high up, near the top of the dash pad. The non-air version was more or less featureless in the same area.

Instruments

Standard Camaro instrumentation in 1969 again consisted of two primary gauge pods.

The left gauge pod was filled with a 120-mile-per-hour speedometer; a 140-mile-per-hour speedometer was used in high-performance models, and the RPO U15 Speed Warning Indicator speedometer was also available. The right gauge pod contained a fuel gauge at the top of the pod, with idiot lights for oil pressure, brake system pressure, and coolant temperature in the lower section.

Between the two gauge pods was a new, small center pod for the optional RPO U35 clock, which no longer had to compete with the optional U16 tachometer for the right pod, nor had to be integrated with it in the infamous "tick-tock-tach."

Speaking of RPO U16, the tach—which actually varied by engine, due to different yellow- and redline settings—was a frequent occupant of the right pod, which displaced the fuel gauge to the RPO U17 Special Instrumentation auxiliary gauge cluster, identical to that of 1968.

Switches and Controls

With the redesigned instrument panel came relocated switches and controls. One of the biggest changes was the new location of the ignition switch: it was located on the right-hand side of the steering column, instead of on the instrument panel as in the past.

Headlamp and windshield wiper (with integrated washer activator) controls were moved low on the left-hand side of the instrument panel. The headlamp switch remained a push-pull–type knob, while a sliding switch was the new way to activate the two-speed wipers. Pushing the wiper lever inward and holding it activated the windshield washer pump.

The left-hand side of the instrument panel also hosted controls for a power convertible top and the rear window defogger, on vehicles so equipped. Those controls were vertical slider-type switches.

The right-hand side of the instrument panel featured three vertical slide levers to control the heating, ventilation, and (if equipped) air conditioning controls. Below those controls is the radio or stereo unit.

The radio and headlight controls featured large round plastic knobs that were chrome plated but featured a blacked-out center.

To the right of the radio, more or less centered in the instrument panel, is a flip-down panel that contains the ashtray and the cigarette lighter.

To the right of the ashtray panel, in front of the passenger seat, is the glovebox. The glovebox door features a "Camaro" script emblem, similar to those found on the car's header and deck lid panels.

Steering Wheels

Three different steering wheels were again available in 1969.

The base wheel was a simple plastic-rimmed wheel with a large rectangular center section that spanned from the three o'clock to nine o'clock positions. In cars with standard interiors, the wheel is black plastic with a pebble-grain faceplate. RPO Z23 and Z87 interiors featured a

wood-grained appliqué on a smooth plastic faceplate to match the wood-grained accents on the instrument panel.

Depending on when and where the car was manufactured, plus other options ordered, the standard steering wheel was equipped with one of four possible center emblems: a Chevy bow tie, a small Camaro script, "RS" lettering, or "SS" lettering. The Z/28 used either the bow tie or Camaro script, unless the RS package was ordered in combination.

Upscale Custom interiors were treated to a simulated walnut dash applique (above). Note that this interior also features the factory tachometer. While the lighting control remained a push-pull knob in 1969 (left), the windshield washer switch changed from a rotating knob to a three-position (off-on-fast) sliding switch that could be pushed to trigger the spray feature.

Washer jets on cars equipped with the RPO CE1 headlight washer system were triggered by this same switch; thus, washing the windshield also washed the headlights.

Controls for the heating and ventilation system were reoriented to a vertical, sliding-switch format. Standard interiors featured a simple black background for most controls, including the radio, below the environmental controls.

The standard SS steering wheel differed little from the base wheel—only the emblem applied was different. Note this car's console, four-speed shifter, and auxiliary gauges.

RPO N34 equipped a Camaro with an attractive and comfortable wood-grained wheel with a brushed-metal three-spoke center. The horn-button cap featured a Chevy "bow tie" logo.

RPO N30, the deluxe padded-rim wheel, featured the same brushed-metal three-spoke center and the same center caps as the N34 wheel.

Steering Columns

Two steering columns were available. The base column, which was included on most cars, was a standard, non-tilting column that served a few different purposes: First and foremost, it transmitted steering inputs to the steering box. Second, the left side of the steering column mounted the turn signal lever switch. Third, on the column's right side was the ignition switch, plus a push-pull switch that controls the hazard indicator lamps.

A tilt column was available under RPO N33. The tilt control lever was located just forward of the turn signal lever and was operated by gently pulling it toward the driver. The column tilted near the instrument panel and provided approximately 6 inches of wheel movement, with detents approximately every inch.

Steering columns were painted to match the instrument panel, which meant they were either body color or black.

The teakwood wheel was a thing of beauty and dressed up any Camaro interior.

Seats

Seats changed again in 1969, but the basic styles were reduced to a single design that included headrests. In base trim, the seats were upholstered in all vinyl. RPO Z87 (Custom Interior) added houndstooth-patterned cloth inserts. In most cases, the fabric was black and white, but black and yellow was available, and the Z10 and Z11 cars used a retina-searing black-and-orange combination! Mercifully removed from the option list was the "Strato-back" front bench seat that never did prove popular for the sporty pony car.

RPO A67 folding rear seat remained on the option list, and nearly 4,400 buyers popped an extra $42.15 for it.

Seat Belts

While the number of seat styles decreased for 1969, the number of seat belt options ballooned to five.

RPO AS1 added front shoulder belts to standard interiors.

RPO AS4 triggered rear shoulder belts to be installed into a Camaro outfitted with the Custom Interior, while RPO AS5 did the same for standard interior coupes.

The ignition switch moved from the instrument panel (in 1967–1968) to the steering column in 1969.

The attractive black-and-white houndstooth fabric seat inserts (below left) were a desirable option in 1969 and continue to be so today. An interesting variation on the houndstooth theme (below): the Indy Pace Car Replicas (Z10, Z11) featured an orange-and-black houndstooth fabric, which matched the orange vinyl, door panels, seat belts, and exterior striping nicely.

Seat belts were color-keyed to match the interior. Several colors were available, including black, orange, blue, and green.

The standard door panel was a simple cardboard base covered with vinyl material. A separate armrest was secured to the door with two screws, and both the door handle and window crank arms were retained by a spring clip.

RPO A39 put Custom Deluxe belts in both the front and rear of convertible models, or RPO A85 could be used to add just front shoulder belts.

Door and Kick Panels

As in the past, both the standard or Custom (RPO Z87) door panel designs were available in 1969. Standard panels were vinyl-covered cardboard with separate padded armrests in matching color.

Custom Interior door panels were a molded design with an integral armrest and a recessed door handle. Custom panels also featured a segment of carpeting along the bottom one-fifth of the panel.

Both door panel designs used the same door lock knobs and the same window crank assemblies. Door release handles differed between the two panel designs. Standard door release handles were long, gently curved, chrome-plated pot metal with a design similar to that of the window crank. Handles for the Custom panels were short, angular, chrome-plated pot metal that more closely resembled the exterior door handles.

Plastic kick panels were color-keyed to the rest of the interior and featured a sliding switch to control airflow through the panels' air vents.

Headliner

Headliners in 1969 Camaros were much like those of 1967 and 1968. Metal support rods span across the top through stitched-in channels in the headliner to help support the headliner. The interior of the C-pillars is covered by cardboard sail panels covered in the same headliner material. Custom Interior cars also feature small round opera lights in the sail panels instead of the standard single dome light normally mounted in the center of the headliner.

Carpet

Once again, Camaros featured two-piece, nylon-blend, loop pile carpet from the factory in 1969. A front piece extends from the firewall rearward to just before the front seats, where it overlaps a rear piece that covers the rest of the floor rearward, ending beneath the rear seat. On the sides, the carpet is secured by the aluminum doorsill trim plates.

Camaro carpets were available in a number of colors to match or contrast with interior trim colors. A small plastic grommet was used to provide a tidy hole around the foot-operated headlamp dimmer switch, and a plastic heel pad was dielectrically bonded to the carpet to prevent wear beneath the driver's feet.

Radios, Tape Players, Speakers, and Antennae

Nineteen sixty-nine Camaro radio equipment was little different from 1967 or 1968.

The U63 and U69 radios played through a single speaker, which was mounted in the center of the instrument panel, beneath a grille in the top of the dash. A second speaker was optional (RPO U80), which was mounted beneath the package shelf behind the rear seat.

RPO U79 played through dual speakers, one mounted in each kick panel behind a unique mesh grille. A multiplex amplifier was mounted higher in the dash. One limitation of RPO U79 was that it was not available with the RPO U80 rear speaker; however, if combined with the U57 8-track system, the stereo system employed four speakers—the two front speakers in the kick panels, plus two more in the rear package tray.

The standard antenna was a fixed-mast unit mounted to the right front fender. RPO U73 was available for those who wanted an antenna mounted to the top of the right rear quarter panel.

RPO U57, Camaro's Stereo (8-track) Tape System, remained a most unusual option. As in the past, the large player unit was mounted atop the console lid, though it was possible (and even prescribed) for the unit to be mounted to the underside of the instrument panel, depending on other options installed.

Console Assembly
RPO D55 was unchanged from 1968 and continued to include a floor-mounted shifter and served as the mounting platform for the RPO U17 Special Instrumentation.

Shifters
For 1969, Camaros were once again available with any one of a number of shifters, depending on the transmission and other options installed. Though rarely installed, column shifters were available for those buyers who didn't want a floor-mounted shifter and were willing to stick with the base three-speed manual or two-speed PowerGlide automatic transmissions. Many optional transmissions included a floor-mounted shifter, some with or without a console.

Manual Transmission Shifter
All manual transmission shifters, whether column mounted or floor mounted, utilized rigid linkage assemblies to convert shifter movements to engagement (or disengagement) of the various transmission gears.

RPO MB1 Torque-Drive transmission was again available for six-cylinder Camaros in 1969. Its shifter was more like those used with the Power Glide automatic than a manual transmission.

RPO M11 added a floor-mounted shifter to Camaros equipped with the base three-speed manual gearbox and a six-cylinder or 327 V-8 engine. This was the same shifter included with the RPO D55 center console.

RPO MC1 replaced RPO M13 as the optional three-speed manual transmission, but continued to include a floor-mounted shifter.

Each of the Muncie four-speed manual transmissions—M20, M21, and the heavy-duty M22— were upgraded for 1969 to include a Hurst shifter and linkage, instead of the flimsy Muncie linkage previously used.

When not equipped with a console, the four-speed shifter assembly was fitted with a black rubber boot, which was secured to the floor with a bright metal trim ring and a number of Phillips-head screws. A black shift knob, imprinted with the shift pattern, was standard.

The same shifter was used in cars equipped with a console, and a black rubber boot was used, but was fastened to the console, rather than the floor. A white shift knob was used on some models, but lacked the shift-pattern imprint; instead the shift pattern was displayed on a small plaque affixed to the console.

Automatic Transmission Shifter
The M35 PowerGlide automatic continued to be supplied with a column-mounted shifter when mated to a six-cylinder engine. The column-mounted shifter was a basic chromed steel rod attached to the right side of the steering column. A small black plastic knob capped the end of the rod.

All console-mounted shifters for automatic transmissions continued to use the "stirrup"-style shifter, which consisted of two chromed vertical posts and a cross-handle with a detent-release button beneath it.

both features, and it became common for Camaro owners to install either the Pontiac or Hurst His-n-Hers shifters.

Pedals

Camaros use either three or four foot-operated pedals, depending on the installed transmission.

Accelerator Pedal

All Camaros use a tall, slender, plastic accelerator pedal attached to a bent steel rod that is hinged on the firewall. The accelerator pedal connects to either mechanical linkages that actuate the carburetor throttle plates, or to a cable that serves the same purpose.

Brake Pedals

All Camaros use a parking brake pedal that is mounted to the underside of the instrument panel, beside the left kick panel. The parking brake pedal assembly features a small, 2-inch pedal with a ribbed rubber pedal pad that has the word "PARK" molded into it. A small release T-handle, with the words "BRAKE RELEASE", is positioned above the pedal assembly, beneath the instrument panel.

All Camaros also have a brake pedal, however, the pedal assemblies are different for models equipped with a manual transmission from those with automatics. Manual transmission cars use a square pedal approximately 3.5 inches wide attached to a thick steel arm suspended from the instrument panel. Automatics use a rectangular pedal roughly 6 inches across. In each case, the pedal sports a ribbed rubber cover. Cars with disc brakes have a small, round metal medallion embedded into the center of the pedal pad. The same brake pedal assemblies were used for non-assisted and power-assisted brakes; the pedal arms featured two mounting holes—one for use with power assist systems, another for use with non-assisted (manual) brakes.

Clutch

Cars equipped with a manual transmission also have a clutch pedal, which is similar to the brake pedal assembly.

Trunk

Camaro trunks are accessed through the deck lid. The trunk itself extends forward, beneath the package shelf, to the back of the rear seatback. The sheet-metal trunk floor was painted in a gray speckled paint with random dots of color, and a vinyl trunk mat with a gray-and-black houndstooth pattern was installed. Unfortunately, the mat often trapped any moisture that entered the trunk, and allowed rust to form beneath it, unseen, usually until it was too late and the trunk floor was ravaged by rust.

Camaros equipped with automatic transmissions featured a stirrup-style shifter with the release button on the underside of the crossbar. Though attractive, the shifter lacked any overshift protection for upshifts and a neutral lock-out mechanism, so was a poor choice for performance driving.

While the factory automatic shifters were perfectly suitable (and stylish) for street use, they lacked a reverse-lockout and upshift detents. Upshift detents would have ensured that any forward upshift (under competition use, at least) would have allowed a driver to move up only one gear at a time (first to second, then second to third). The reverse lockout would have functioned similarly, but prevented drivers from accidentally shifting into reverse no matter how hard they tried. Pontiac provided a version of Hurst's "His-n-Hers" shifter, which provided

The trunk is rather featureless. The only points of interest are the spare tire, jack equipment, and lug wrench, plus optional equipment and the convertible top "cocktail shaker" vibration dampers.

Spare Tire

Spare tires were of the same size and make as those installed on the vehicle. The wheel on which the spare tire was mounted was typically a base steel wheel, and lies with the face (front) of the wheel down. The jack equipment is stowed inside and beneath the spare tire assembly.

RPO N65, the "Space-Saver" spare tire and wheel, again went largely unnoticed as only 2,228 buyers ordered the unique, space-saving option.

Jack Equipment

Camaros were equipped with a multipiece set of jack equipment, which included the jack post, jack base, the ratcheting load rest bracket, the lug wrench, a screwdriver, a retaining bolt, and a wing nut.

The jack post had a cadmium-plated finish, while the load rest bracket and base were painted semigloss black and the retaining bolt and wing nut were given a zinc-oxide finish. The lug wrench was either painted semigloss black or given a zinc-oxide finish, depending on the time of year and manufacturing plant. Different screwdrivers were used, depending on the time of year and manufacturing plant.

Convertible Top Equipment

Convertible Top Vibration Dampers resemble large cocktail shakers, approximately 5 inches in diameter and 10 inches tall. One was installed in each corner of the car because the Camaro convertible body structure was considerably weaker than the coupe, due to the lack of the roof, so the body flexed and vibrated more. The vibration dampers were an attempt to minimize the unwanted body movements. The dampers were installed prior to the trunk being painted at the factory, so they typically feature trunk paint overspray.

Instructional Decals

A number of instructional and information decals were affixed to the underside of the Camaro deck lid. The exact number of decals varies with the specific options installed. All Camaros featured a jacking instruction decal; limited-slip Positraction differential (RPO G80), Rally wheels (RPO ZJ7), and others each added a decal to the deck lid.

Powertrain

If it wasn't already clear by 1969 that the Camaro was a true performance car, then there was certainly no mistaking it by the end of the year.

For 1969, there were two six-cylinder engines, six small-block V-8s, plus another six Mark IV big-block V-8s, for a total of 14 engines. Naturally, each engine was generally available with a choice of transmissions, which made for a dizzying array of combinations.

In addition, the 10- and 12-bolt rear axle assemblies each continued to be available with or without Positraction (limited-slip) differentials and a range of gear ratios; a new option for 1969 even added Corvette-style disc brakes to the rear axle assembly.

Engines

While the six-cylinder lineup remained the same as in 1968, the base V-8 started out the same but then changed when Chevrolet introduced its new 307-ci V-8. Optional 327s were nixed prior to the beginning of the 1969 model year production, which was actually good news, given the value of the trio of 350s that were available. Even the Z/28 302 underwent a number of changes to improve it (for competition use).

The Mark IV engine line also changed, though few people were ever aware of it at the time. Two COPOs were available to those who knew of them, each of which featured a limited-production 427-ci Mark IV V-8.

But the changes weren't limited to only the new engines. All the V-8 engines received new accessory drive systems that positioned the alternator on the right-hand side of the engine. Engines equipped with an Air Injection Reactor (AIR)

The trunk of a typical 1969 Camaro featured a spare tire and the assorted jacking equipment, all neatly stowed. Unfortunately, the standard spare tire consumed much of the limited trunk space available, leaving little room for packages. An inflatable "Space-Saver" spare tire was available under RPO N65, which helped reclaim otherwise wasted space.

The 350-ci Chevy V-8, originally introduced in the Camaro in 1967, had become a mainstay of Chevy's powerplant lineup by 1969. Several 350s were available for the Camaro, including 225-, 250-, and 300-horsepower variations. This one features incorrect Z/28-style finned aluminum valve covers. The 350s were, however, frequently equipped with chrome valve covers and air cleaner lids to dress up the engine compartment appearance.

pump also had it mounted to the right-hand side of the engine. Air conditioning and power steering systems were mounted to the left-hand side of the engine.

I-6 Engines

A 140-horsepower 230-ci inline six-cylinder was the base engine, again, while RPO L22 also carried over to 1969 as the only optional six-gun: a 250-ci model with 155 horsepower. Buyers were mostly torn between the two six-cylinder engines: 17,588 stuck with the base engine, while 18,660 went all out for the $26.35 optional six.

V-8 Small-Block Engines

The small-block engines continued to be the versatile engine family in 1969. On the low end was the economical base V-8, which started out as the same 215-horsepower 327 as used in 1968 and changed after the start of production to a 210-horsepower 307-ci small-block. Optional 225- and 250-horsepower 350s provided modest performance across the board, while the 300-horsepower

350 and the 290-horsepower Z28 302 each packed an incredible power punch for their size and price.

As before, the small-block V-8s looked largely the same, except for cosmetic differences such as air cleaner assemblies, valve covers, and induction systems. Another new feature for 1969 was the switch to a new "long"-style water pump, which made the new pulley systems and accessory mounting locations possible.

Base 327 small-block engines were unchanged for 1969 from the previous year. Air was ingested through and mixed with fuel in a two-barrel Rochester carburetor that bolted to a simple, cast-iron intake manifold. An 8.75:1 compression ratio and a mild hydraulic camshaft kept the engine fuel-efficient while helping it develop 210 horsepower. As good as the base 327 was at performing its job, Chevy replaced the engine during the production year with its new 307-ci V-8.

Base 307 small-block engines were introduced in January 1969. The hope was that the 307—which featured a slightly smaller bore but the same 3.25-inch stroke of the 327—would be

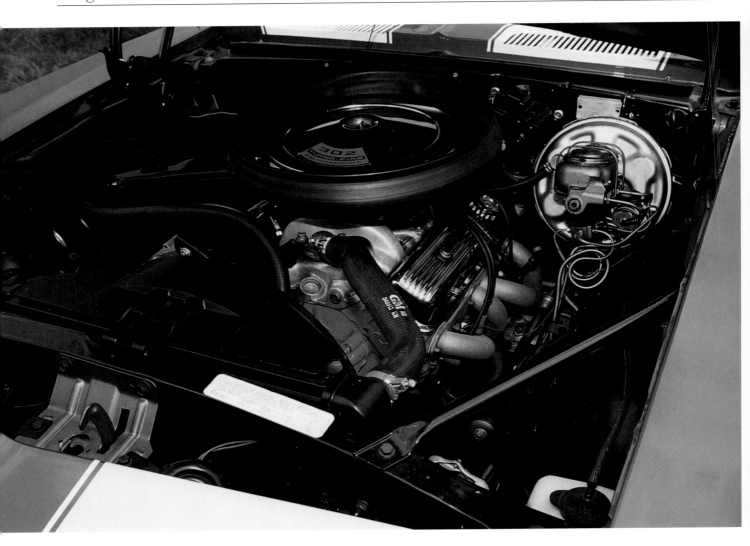

more fuel-efficient. It was, but only marginally. Unfortunately, the engine's dimensions were not well suited to performance use.

RPO LM1 was offered at the start of the season as a low-cost upgrade V-8. But the engine was dropped during the production year to simplify Chevy's engine lineup between its various models. RPO L65 replaced it.

RPO L48 changed only minimally for 1969. Aside from the new pulley configuration and some minor "trim" changes, some tuning tweaks boosted output by 5 horsepower to 300. The L48 remained the base SS engine, and the top of the small-block heap.

RPO L65, which replaced the 225-horsepower LM1 350, was already available in other Chevrolet models and developed 250 horsepower. Fed by a Rochester QuadraJet and an iron intake, the engine offered good performance, decent economy, and impressive reliability for a measly $21.10. Chevy sold 26,898 L65-equipped Camaros in 1969.

RPO Z28 was hardly a secret by 1969. Sales had grown from just 602 in 1967 to 7,199 for 1968. Another astounding jump to 20,302 units came in 1969, based in no small part on the feisty 302, which had already earned quite a reputation for itself—on the track and off. And for 1969, the 302 was better than ever. While the forged crank and rods were beefed up in 1968 with larger journals, the block was given four-bolt main bearing caps on the middle three journals. The four-bolt caps not only kept the crankshaft more securely located, but also minimized any flexing of the block. While an open-element air cleaner assembly was standard on the Z28's 302, the new ZL2 "cowl induction" hood was available on the Z28 and added an air cleaner base that sealed to the hood with a foam-rubber seal to draw cold air from the outside. In addition, a unique "Cross-Ram" induction system was available, which utilized two 600-cfm Holley four-barrel carburetors on a boxlike aluminum intake. As the name suggested, the right carburetor fed the left bank of cylinders,

The awesome 302 of the Z/28 Camaro was often combined with the ZL2 "cowl induction" hood, which fed the engine cool outside air through the hood's scoop and the special air cleaner base assembly that sealed to the underside of the hood. This 302 is equipped with aftermarket exhaust headers; all 302s shipped from the factory with log-style, cast-iron exhaust manifolds.

A wild upgrade available only on the Z/28's 302 was the ominous Cross-Ram intake, which mounted dual 600-cfm Holley four-barrel carburetors atop a short-runner, larger-plenum aluminum intake. The Cross-Ram nickname came from the fact that each carburetor fed the opposite bank of cylinders.

The now-legendary "Z/28" emblem was included as part of RPO Z28.

while the left carburetor fed the right bank. Other subtle tweaks, including the new accessory drive system, increased engine durability and reliability.

V-8 Big-Block Engines
"Officially," the big-block options for 1969 were no different (apart from new accessory drive

systems and water pumps) from those of 1968—four healthy 396s: the L34, L35, L78, and L89 396s. Unofficially, there were two additional choices: the COPO 427s. The L72 427 was rated at 435 horsepower and was essentially a big-inch version of the L78. The ZL1 427, on the other hand, was rated at just 425 horsepower, but featured an ultralight aluminum block and heads—and a $4,160 option price!

The L72 427 was available under COPO 9561 for $489.45 (and was often combined with COPO 9737, the Sports Car Conversion package, which added another $184.70) and was the foundation of many dealers' 427 "conversion" Camaros, including Yenko, Berger, and others. There is no concrete evidence of just how many 9561 COPO Camaros were produced, but it is known that 193 code MN (automatic) and 822 code MO (manual) L72 427s were produced, and that a percentage of those were done for warranty and repair purposes, so the true figure is that something less than 1,015 (most likely around 800, given typical for-warranty production percentages) COPO 9561 Camaros were built.

The ZL1, which was listed as part of COPO 9560, was Chevy's attempt to improve the Camaro's performance in drag racing competition, plain and simple. The company certainly didn't intend to sell many $8,000 Camaros to the public; they were intended for racers, for whom the price tag could be justified. In the end, just 69 ZL1 Camaros (47 manuals, 22 automatics) were built, plus two ZL1 Corvettes. A handful of extra engines were assembled; although records have not confirmed this, it is believed 88 ZL1 engines were built.

Transmissions

The only noteworthy change to Camaro transmission offerings for 1969 was an RPO code change. RPO M13, which had signified a heavy-duty three-speed manual gearbox in 1967 and 1968, was changed to RPO MC1 for 1969. The transmission itself was nothing remarkable, however.

All other transmissions remained available, and received only typical minor modifications from the previous year to improve durability.

Driveshafts

Though hardly perfection, the typical steel tube driveshafts used in 1967 and 1968 were effective and economical, and needed only the most subtle refinements for the new year. Since only the Camaro's bodywork had changed for 1969, the actual wheelbase was the same (108 inches), so driveshafts remained the same length as before.

Rear Axle Assemblies

Rear axle assemblies are yet another largely unchanged component of 1969 Camaros. The trusted 10- and 12-bolt Saginaw rear ends had each proven themselves worthy of serving Camaro owners, be they tender-footed elderly buyers, torturous racers, or, more than likely, somewhere in between.

One change for 1969 that did affect the rear axle housing assembly was the availability of a from-the-factory four-wheel disc brake option, under RPO JL8. Because of the different brake system equipment at the end of each axle, the axles had to be

The base L35 396 was rated at 325 horsepower, which made it more than a match for many challengers. This L35 is installed in a Z11 Indy Pace Car Replica.

The L34 396 boasted an additional 25 horsepower over the L35, but cost $120 more. Only 2,018 buyers justified the imbalanced cost-per-horsepower ratio. Note that this L34 is equipped with a non-stock black-finished air cleaner lid; stock lids were chrome plated.

shortened, which in turn necessitated narrower axle tubes. It should also be noted that GM offered a service replacement four-wheel discbrake –equipped rear end for Camaros and Firebirds that differed from the factory-installed rear end by way of heavier-duty (larger-diameter) axles that were shot-peened and magnafluxed to ensure durability.

Chassis

As with most other "under-the-skin" elements of the 1969 Camaro, its chassis was almost indistinguishable from the 1967–1968 semi-unitized chassis structure.

Body Structure

Apart from new quarter panels, the 1969 body structure received no significant changes from 1968, which meant the 1969 Camaros have essentially the same strengths and weaknesses as earlier models.

Subframe Assembly

The subframe assembly was updated for 1969 to accommodate the changed front-end sheet metal and other minor revisions. As in the past, however, it was provided with only a light coating of rust preventative.

Floor Pan

The Camaro's floor pan, like the basic body structure of which it is an integral part, didn't change for 1969, nor did the reinforcement plate for convertibles. All panels featured a bare metal finish treated with a temporary rust preventative.

Wheels and Tires

A number of different wheel and tire combinations were available in 1969, giving plenty of options for budget-minded buyers and racers alike.

As before, all wheels were made of welded stamped steel in a variety of widths and two diameters. Many wheels were designed for use with full wheel covers or smaller center-caps (with or without trim rings).

Different tire suppliers were used throughout the 1968 model year, depending on the size and

style tire, and depending on the available supply. In addition, the tires installed often varied between the two Camaro assembly plants in Norwood, Ohio, and Los Angeles, California.

Wheels
A third wheel design joined the base steel wheel and the slotted Rally wheel: the new Super Sport wheel, which was based on the Kelsey-Hayes "Magnum 500" five-spoke-styled steel wheel.

The base wheel measured 14.0x5.5 inches. Non-Z28 Rally wheels and the new SS wheels measured 14.0x7.0 inches, while the Z28 initially used the 1968 Z28 15.0x6.0-inch version of the Rally wheel, then switched to a 15.0x7.0-inch wheel when the supply of narrower wheels was depleted. All Rally wheels come with bright trim rings and turbine-style center caps. Super Sport wheels also featured bright trim rings and small center caps with the "SS" logo on them.

Tires
A number of different tire makes, models, styles, and sizes were installed on Camaros at the two factories throughout the model year.

The majority of 1969 Camaros rolled around on E78x14 tires, whether blackwall or the optional (RPO PK8) whitewall tires. The remaining lineup of tires was the same as 1968. Z28s rolled away on E70x15 nylon tires.

Suspension
Camaro suspension changes for 1969 were limited to slightly revised shock valving and spring rates. In fact, the biggest change of 1969 was the availability of large-diameter (1-inch) front stabilizer ("sway") bars. The standard stabilizer bar for 1969 was the same size—11/16 inch—as the Z28 bar from 1967–1968. Meanwhile, the 1969 Z28 bar increased to 13/16 inch. And an even larger 1-inch bar was available as part of COPO 9737, the Sports Car Conversion option.

The remainder of the 1969 Camaro suspension system was largely the same as the 1968 system, including the lack of a rear anti-roll bar.

Brakes
Drum brakes were standard equipment at all four corners, though many options added disc brakes to either the front wheels or even all four wheels in 1969.

The top gun in the Camaro engine lineup (on paper, anyway) is the 435-horsepower 427 big-block installed by the factory for those buyers knowledgeable enough to order COPO #9561.

The ultimate Camaro engine—ever!—is the legendary ZL1 427 with its exotic aluminum block and cylinder heads. Chevy rated the engine at 425 horsepower in hopes of pulling the wool over the National Hot Rod Association's eyes. It didn't work. But it also didn't really matter. Only 69 buyers figured out how to get one: by ordering COPO 9560 and shelling out over $4,000 for the engine alone (on top of the Camaro's nearly $3,000 base price)!

The basic components of the 1969 brake systems were nearly identical to those of 1968: a natural-finish cast-iron master cylinder, natural-finish steel lines, steel-strand cables inside a spiral-wound sheath of natural-finished steel, and rubber-covered flexible high-pressure hoses at each front wheel and one for both rear wheels.

Disc brake hardware also changed for 1969.

Front and Rear Drum Brakes

Once again, four-wheel drum brakes were standard equipment on 1969 Camaros. The drums had a semigloss black finish, as did the steel backing plates and the wheel cylinders.

RPO J50 added a vacuum-operated power assist to the drum brake system to reduce the brake pedal effort necessary to operate the brake system. The booster unit is a circular, steel vacuum diaphragm assembly mounted between the master cylinder and the firewall. The booster unit featured a gold-hued cadmium-plated finish. Power brake–equipped Camaros utilize different master cylinders from those without power brakes. In addition, the brake pedal assembly uses a different hinge point than non–power brake systems.

RPO J52 Front Disc/Rear Drum Brakes

The benefits of disc brakes were already common knowledge by 1969. RPO J52 added front disc brakes to any Camaro, though several options included RPO J52 hardware, including the Super Sports and Z28. While disc brakes had been available in the past, the design was significantly improved for 1969. Instead of the leak-prone four-piston Corvette-inspired calipers, the 1969 Camaro system used a new single-piston design with revised seals that virtually eliminated leaks and reduced pad wear.

RPO JL8 Four-Wheel Disc Brakes

For the first time, four-wheel disc brakes were available on a Camaro from the factory. The system added 11.75-inch disc brake rotors to the front wheels, and same-size rotors to the rear wheels. Four-piston calipers were used at all four corners to grasp the rotors. Interestingly enough, the system did not utilize a proportioning valve, though many owners purchased a Kelsey-Hayes adjustable valve, which was available through GM's parts chain, to adjust their front-to-rear brake bias.

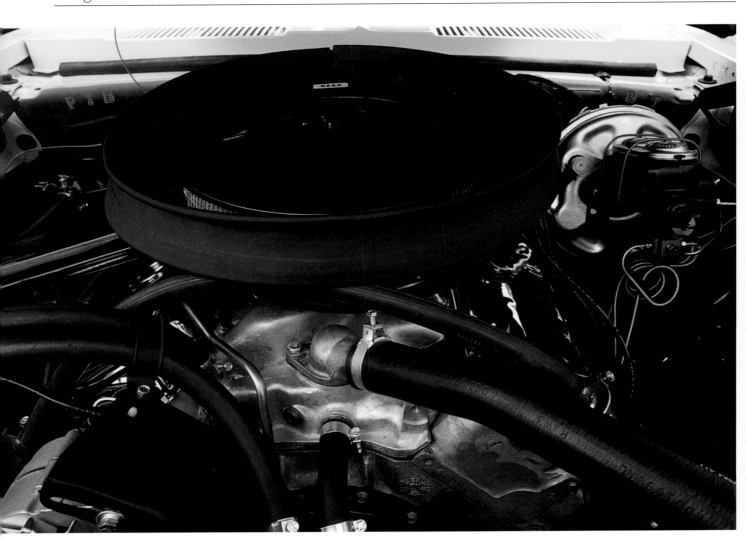

Rear disc brake kits had been available in the past, through GM dealers' parts departments.

Steering

In appearance, Camaro steering systems and components didn't change much for 1969. But yank the steering wheel one way or the other and you would instantly notice a difference. Internally, the steering box was updated with a new variable-ratio gear set that provided better steering feel, especially as speeds increased.

The steering wheels remained large by today's standards: 16 inches in diameter for the standard wheel, and a similar size for the optional wheels. The large wheel increased the driver's leverage, which reduced steering effort, but at the expense of steering feel.

Both the standard steering column and the RPO N33 tilt columns remained available. However, both now included an ignition switch on their right-hand side. As in the past, the columns were painted to match the interior color scheme.

RPO N40 added power steering to either the base steering system or the RPO N44 quick-ratio steering system. Although the pulley and pump mounting brackets were revised to work with the new accessory drive system, the items were similar to 1968.

There were several different steering boxes available, each of which mounted to the left sub-frame rail between the front cross-member and the firewall, and featured a natural cast-iron finish with a natural-finished aluminum access cover. Standard was a non-assisted manual unit with a 24:1 gear ratio and linkage that resulted in a 28.3:1 overall ratio. RPO N44 quick-ratio steering yielded a 21.4:1 overall ratio, while Z/28s with RPO N44 provided a much lower 17.9:1 overall ratio for a far better feel and at-speed action.

Ordering RPO N40 provided a variable-ratio, engine-driven, hydraulic power steering assist. Without RPO N44, RPO N40 featured a 16.1:1 ratio on-center (15.5:1 overall) that reduced to a 12.4:1 ratio at full-lock. The same steering box was

This close-up of the ZL1 shows the Winters Foundry snowflake casting mark in the cylinder block above the timing cover. An aluminum water pump housing was also included with the ZL1 engine. The aluminum color made the engine stand out under the hood, compared to the typical Chevy Orange big-blocks. Its power made it stand out on the racetrack.

The Z/28 became almost a commodity in 1969, selling 20,302 copies. Those buyers were rewarded for waiting to get a Z: the 302 engine was structurally strengthened, plus the car received wider wheels and tires to improve handling. This Z28 is also equipped with the revised Rally Sport package. Note that the period-correct aftermarket wheels were not available from the factory.

used for cars equipped with both RPOs N40 and N44, but differences in the steering linkage resulted in a higher-effort 14.3:1 overall ratio on-center.

As in the past, a natural-finish cast-iron pitman arm connects the steering box output shaft to the parallel relay rod (more commonly called a "drag link" or "center link"), which is supported at the right subframe rail by the idler arm. The ends of the relay rod connect to inner tie-rod ends. Tie-rod adjustment sleeves connect the inner tie-rod ends to the outer tie-rod ends, which connect to the steering knuckles. The relay rod, idler arm, tie-rod ends, and steering knuckles were all natural-finished cast iron, while the tie-rod adjustment sleeves were natural-finished steel.

Fuel System

The biggest change to Camaro fuel systems in 1969 was that nearly all V-8 intake manifolds (small- and big-block alike) were revised for 1969. In most cases, the changes were minor, such as the relocated thermostat housing on the aluminum

high-rise Z28 intake (#3932472). In addition, the oil fill tube was deleted from all engines and a freeze plug was installed in the fill-tube mounting hole. Oil fill provisions were provided in the right-hand rocker cover.

A less significant change to Camaro fuel systems in 1969 was the relocation of the fuel filler inlet from the rear taillamp panel to behind a flip-down license plate frame. The change necessitated a different fuel tank.

The various fuel lines, fuel pumps, fuel filters, and other components were, again, essentially unchanged. The steel fuel lines continued to have a natural finish, while the fuel pump's aluminum housing also featured a natural finish, but with some engine paint overspray at the pump's base.

Like the intake manifolds, several carburetors were slightly revised for 1969, resulting in new list and model numbers. All carburetors, however, continued to feature a gold cadmium-plated finish on their aluminum bodies and other components. The

finish was quickly tarnished, however, and resulted in a dingy-gray appearance. Fuel leaks only hastened any degradation of the carburetor's appearance.

Exhaust System

Most Camaro exhaust systems were similar in 1969 to their 1968 counterparts in materials (low-grade steel tubing), finish (natural), and configuration. There was one unique new exhaust system option in 1969: RPO NC8's chambered exhaust, which was only available with SS or Z28 equipment (and was included with Z28s built in the last two months of 1968).

The NC8 system didn't utilize traditional matt-packed mufflers, but rather featured double-walled pipes. The inner pipe, which carried the exhaust gases, was perforated to the outer pipe. The outer pipe, meanwhile, was crimped into multiple sections of varying length along one length of pipe. The different-sized chambers were intended to filter out different exhaust noise frequencies without the need for any sound-absorbing mats. The chambered exhaust system proved to be excessively loud and was actually illegal in

many states. Consequently, it was dropped from production in June 1969.

Camaro exhaust systems were simple and largely typical for the day: natural-finish (with some overspray near the cylinder heads) cast-iron exhaust manifolds collected gases from the engine and then funneled them to individual "header" pipes. For single-exhaust systems, the left-hand header pipe crossed between the subframe cross-member and the oil pan sump to merge with the right-hand pipe to feed the intermediate pipe. The intermediate pipe ran rearward inside the transmission tunnel, then swept up and over the left-hand side of the rear axle assembly and into a single transverse-mounted muffler. A single tailpipe exited the right-hand side of the muffler, curved rearward, and dumped the exhaust gases out beneath the rear lower valance panel.

RPO NF2, 1968's deep-tone exhaust, became 1969's RPO N10 dual-exhaust system. At different times throughout the year, and with different engines, the N10 system utilized a number of different tailpipes. In some cases, the tailpipes exited immediately behind the rear tires and

The "dog dish" or "poverty caps" wheel covers (above left) are actually prized by collectors today, partially because so few cars were equipped with them. The wheels were plain steel painted to match the body. A number of tire makes and models were used throughout 1969, and in fact the actual equipment installed varied between the Van Nuys and Norwood plants, based on what was available at the time. This Goodyear Polyglas tire (above right) is mounted on the optional Rally wheel with its turbine-style center cap and bright trim ring.

Super Sports in 1969 received a new wheel, based on the Kelsey-Hayes "Magnum 500" wheel. The steel wheel has five primary ribs plus recessed coves that were painted black in 1969.

Air conditioning equipment consumed a large chunk of the right-hand side of the firewall, when ordered.

pointed downward. On SS and Z28 models, in particular, the tailpipes were much longer and actually exited beneath the rear valance panel, parallel to the ground.

Again, all exhaust pipes and mufflers were natural-finished mild steel and were quite prone to rusting. Header and intermediate pipe diameters remained conservative: single-exhaust and small-block (except Z/28) dual-exhaust systems were comprised of pipes that measured 2.0 inches, while Z/28 and 396 dual-exhaust systems utilized 2.25-inch pipes for increased flow capacity and efficiency. Tailpipes measured 2 inches in diameter, regardless of the system.

Contrary to popular opinion, the 1969 Z28 was not available with tubular steel exhaust headers, as in 1968.

Cooling System

With so little different about the 1969 Camaro's mechanical systems, there was little reason for Chevrolet to reengineer the car's cooling systems.

The most noticeable difference was hardly noticeable at all: a new, "long" water pump that allowed for a redesigned, more durable accessory drive system.

The thermostat outlets were relocated slightly on several intake manifolds, and the housings were often different from those used in 1968, depending on options installed on the car.

Engine Cooling System

The engine cooling system used the same basic components and combinations of them as used since 1967. Radiators with two rows, three rows, and four rows of cooling tubes were used for the low-, medium-, and high-performance applications, respectively. The RPO V01 heavy-duty radiator added the next radiator size up from a model's standard radiator, while most air-conditioned (RPO C60) cars were equipped with three-row radiators.

Again depending on the radiator and other options, a partial or full fan shroud was installed to improve safety and cooling efficiency. Likewise, a number of fans were available, differing in blade count, material, and whether they featured a viscous fan clutch or not. All of these items were similar or identical to their 1967 counterparts.

Passenger Cooling System

The heating, ventilation, and air conditioning systems were also much as they were in 1967, though they benefited from new outlets near the sides of the instrument panel. As before, a number of heating and cooling options were available, from the RPO C50 rear window defroster to full heater/defroster deletes (which had to be manually written on the order form).

Appendices

APPENDIX A
DECODING 1967–1969 CAMARO VEHICLE IDENTIFICATION NUMBER (VIN) PLATES

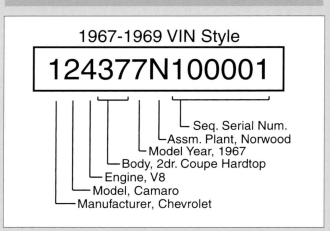

1967-1969 VIN Style

124377N100001

- Seq. Serial Num.
- Assm. Plant, Norwood
- Model Year, 1967
- Body, 2dr. Coupe Hardtop
- Engine, V8
- Model, Camaro
- Manufacturer, Chevrolet

1967–1969 CAMARO VIN CODES

Example: 124377N100637

Character	Data Type	Possibilities
1	Make	1 = Chevrolet
2	Model	2 = Camaro
3	Engine	3 = 6 cylinder 4 = 8 cylinder
4	Body Type	3 = Hardtop 6 = Convertible
5	Bodystyle	7 = 2-door Coupe
6	Model Year	7 = 1967 8 = 1968 9 = 1969
7	Assembly Plant	N = Norwood, OH L = Van Nuys, CA
8–13	Unit Number	Sequential Number per plant, per year 1967 Starts: 100001 1968 Starts: 300001 1969 Starts: 500001

APPENDIX B
DECODING 1967–1969 CAMARO TRIM PLATES

1967 CAMARO TRIM PLATE CODES

Location	Data	Code(s)	Description/Note(s)
A	Build Month	01	January
		02	February
		03	March
		04	April
		05	May
		06	June
		07	July
		08	August
		09	September
		10	October
		11	November
		12	December
B	Build Week	A	1st Week
		B	2nd Week
		C	3rd Week
		D	4th Week
		E	5th Week
C	Interior Color*	B	Blue
		D	Red
		E	Black
		G	Gold
		K	Parchment/Black
		R	Bright Blue
		T	Turquoise
	*Norwood only	Y	Yellow
D	Production Tracking Number		Internal plant code used at Van Nuys only. The letter indicates a manufacturing period and the number indicates the unit production during that period.

Location	Data	Code(s)	Description/Note(s)
E	Model Year	67	1967
F	Interior Style	12437	Sport Coupe, standard interior
		12467	Convertible, standard interior
		12637	Sport Coupe, custom interior
		12667	Convertible, custom interior
G	Assembly Plant	LOS	Van Nuys (Los Angeles), CA
		NOR	Norwood, OH
H	Body Unit Number		Sequential body build number
I	Interior Trim	707	Yellow custom buckets
		709	Gold standard buckets
		711	Gold custom buckets
		712	Gold custom bench
		716	Bright Blue custom bench
		717	Blue standard buckets
		732	Bright Blue custom buckets
		739	Blue standard bench
		741	Red standard buckets
		742	Red custom buckets
		756	Black standard bench
		760	Black standard buckets
		765	Black custom buckets
		767	Black custom bench
		779	Turquoise custom buckets
		796	Gold standard bench
		797	Parchment custom buckets
		Z	Custom bucket seat trim
		H	Bench seat
		Y	Headrests
J	Lower Body Color	A	Tuxedo Black
		C	Ermine White
		D	Nantucket Blue

Location	Data	Code(s)	Description/Note(s)
		E	Deepwater Blue
		F	Marina Blue
		G	Granada Gold
		H	Mountain Green
		K	Emerald Turquoise
		M	Royal Plum
		N	Madeira Maroon
		R	Bolero Red
		S	Sierra Fawn
		T	Capri Cream
		Y	Butternut Yellow
K	Upper Body, Convertible, or Vinyl Top Color	1	White Fabric
		2	Black Fabric
		A	Tuxedo Black
		C	Ermine White
		D	Nantucket Blue
		E	Deepwater Blue
		F	Marina Blue
		G	Granada Gold
		H	Mountain Green
		K	Emerald Turquoise
		M	Royal Plum
		N	Madeira Maroon
		R	Bolero Red
		S	Sierra Fawn
		T	Capri Cream
		Y	Butternut Yellow
L	Group 1 Options	D	Power Convertible Top
		E	Tinted Windows, All
		L	Fold-Down Rear Seat
		X	Power Windows
		W	Tinted Windshield
M	Group 2 Options	B	3-spd w/floor shifter
		E	Air Conditioning (C60)
		G	Center Consol
		H	Heater Delete
		L	4-spd w/floor shifter
		M	Powerglide
		R	Rear Seat Speaker
		S	Rear Antenna
		U	8-track player/Multiplex

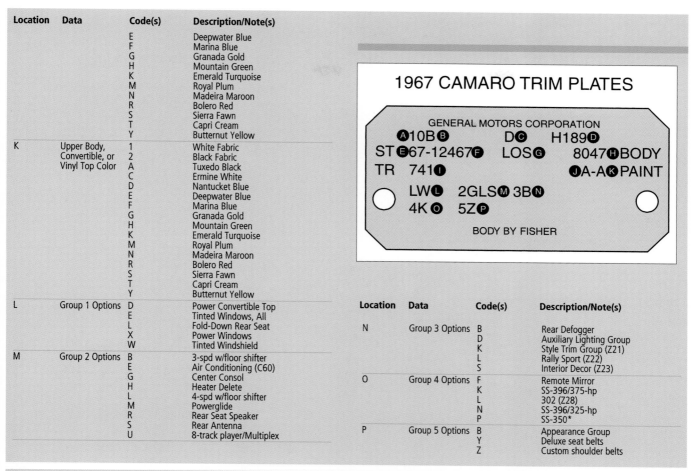

1967 CAMARO TRIM PLATES

GENERAL MOTORS CORPORATION
Ⓐ10BⒷ   DⒸ   H189Ⓓ
STⒺ67-12467Ⓕ   LOSⒼ   8047ⒽBODY
TR 741Ⓘ   ⒿA-AⓀPAINT
LWⓁ   2GLSⓂ 3BⓃ
4KⓄ   5ZⓅ
BODY BY FISHER

Location	Data	Code(s)	Description/Note(s)
N	Group 3 Options	B	Rear Defogger
		D	Auxiliary Lighting Group
		K	Style Trim Group (Z21)
		L	Rally Sport (Z22)
		S	Interior Decor (Z23)
O	Group 4 Options	F	Remote Mirror
		K	SS-396/375-hp
		L	302 (Z28)
		N	SS-396/325-hp
		P	SS-350*
P	Group 5 Options	B	Appearance Group
		Y	Deluxe seat belts
		Z	Custom shoulder belts

1968 CAMARO TRIM PLATE CODES

Location	Data	Code(s)	Description/Note(s)
A	Build Month	01	January
		02	February
		03	March
		04	April
		05	May
		06	June
		07	July
		08	August
		09	September
		10	October
		11	November
		12	December
B	Build Week	A	1st Week
		B	2nd Week
		C	3rd Week
		D	4th Week
		E	5th Week
C	Production Tracking Number	Internal plant code used at Van Nuys only. The letter indicates a manufacturing period and the number indicates the unit production during that period.	
D	Model Year	68	1968
E	Model Type	12337	Sport Coupe, 6-cylinder
		12367	Convertible, 6-cylinder
		12437	Sport Coupe, 8-cylinder
		12467	Convertible, 8-cylinder
F	Assembly Plant	LOS	Van Nuys (Los Angeles), CA
		NOR	Norwood, OH
G	Body Unit Number	Sequential body build number	
H	Interior Trim	711	Ivory custom buckets
		712	Black standard buckets

Location	Data	Code(s)	Description/Note(s)
		713	Black standard bench
		714	Black custom buckets
		715	Black custom bench
		716	Ivory/Houndstooth buckets
		717	Blue standard buckets
		718	Blue standard bench
		719	Blue custom buckets
		720	Blue custom bench
		721	Gold custom buckets
		722	Gold standard buckets
		723	Gold standard bench
		724	Red standard buckets
		725	Red custom buckets
		726	Turquoise custom buckets
		727	Turquoise custom bench
		730	Parchment custom buckets
		749	Black/Houndstooth buckets
I	Lower Body Color	A	Tuxedo Black
		C	Ermine White
		D	Grotto Blue
		E	Fathom Blue
		F	Island Teal
		G	Ash Gold
		H	Grecian Green
		J	Rallye Green
		K	Tripoli Turquoise
		L	Teal Blue
		N	Cordovan Maroon
		O	Corvette Bronze
		P	Seafrost Green
		R	Matador Red
		T	Palomino Ivory
		U	LeMans Blue
		V	Sequoia Green
		Y	Butternut Yellow
		Z	British Green
		(blank) or - -	Special Order Paint

Location	Data	Code(s)	Description/Note(s)
J	Upper Body, Convertible, or Vinyl Top Color	1	White convertible top
		2	Black conv. or vinyl top
		4	Blue convertible top
		6	White vinyl top
		A	Tuxedo Black
		C	Ermine White
		D	Grotto Blue
		E	Fathom Blue
		F	Island Teal
		G	Ash Gold
		H	Grecian Green
		J	Rallye Green
		K	Tripoli Turquoise
		L	Teal Blue
		N	Cordovan Maroon
		O	Corvette Bronze
		P	Seafrost Green
		R	Matador Red
		T	Palomino Ivory
		U	LeMans Blue
		V	Sequoia Green
		Y	Butternut Yellow
		Z	British Green

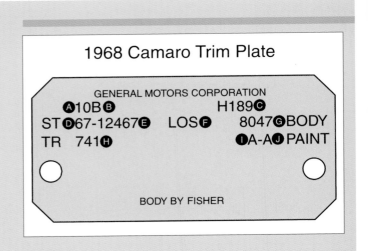

1969 CAMARO TRIM PLATE CODES

Location	Data	Code(s)	Description/Note(s)
A	Model ID	12337	Sport Coupe, 6-cylinder
		12367	Convertible, 8-cylinder
		12437	Sport Coupe, 8-cylinder
		12467	Convertible, 8-cylinder
B	Assembly Plant	N O R	Norwood, OH
		V N	Van Nuys (Los Angeles), CA
C	Body Unit Number	Sequential body build number	
D	Interior Trim	711	Black standard
		712	Black custom
		713	Black/Houndstooth
		714	Yellow/Houndstooth
		715	Blue standard
		716	Blue custom
		718	Red standard
		719	Red custom
		720	Orange/Houndstooth
		721	Medium Green standard
		722	Medium Green custom
		723	Midnight Green standard
		725	Midnight Green custom
		727	Ivory standard
		729	Ivory/Houndstooth
		A	White convertible top
		B	Black convertible top
E / F	Lower/Upper Body Colors and/or Fabric	10	Tuxedo Black
		50	Dover White
		51	Dusk Blue
		52	Garnet Red
		53	Glacier Blue
		55	Azure Turquoise
		57	Fathom Green
		59	Frost Green
		61	Burnished Brown
		65	Olympic Gold
		67	Burgundy
		69	Cortez Silver
		71	LeMans Blue
		72	Hugger Orange
		76	Daytona Yellow
		79	Rallye Green
		B	Black vinyl top
		C	Blue vinyl top
		E	Parchment vinyl top
		F	Brown vinyl top
		S	Green vinyl top
		(blank) or - -	Special Order Paint
G	Build Month	1	January
		2	February
		3	March
		4	April
		5	May
		6	June

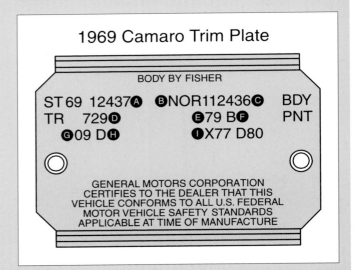

Location	Data	Code(s)	Description/Note(s)
		7	July
		8	August
		9	September
		10	October
		11	November
		12	December
H	Build Week	A	1st week
		B	2nd week
		C	3rd week
		D	4th week
		E	5th week
I*	Exterior Trim	D80	F&R Spoilers**
		X11	Style Trim Group
		X22	Style Trim w/SS-396
		X33	Style Trim w/Z28
		X44	Base model
		X55	Base w/Z27
		X66	Base w/SS-396
		X77	Base w/Z28
		Z10	Indy Pace Car Accents, Coupe
		Z11	Indy Pace Car Accents, Conv.

*Norwood late style only, VINs N544001 to end of production
**Not coded on all D80-equipped cars

APPENDIX C
REGULAR PRODUCTION OPTION (RPO) AND CENTRAL OFFICE PRODUCTION ORDER (COPO) CODES

RPO/COPO	Description	1967 Model Year		1968 Model Year		1969 Model Year	
		Price ($)	Production	Price ($)	Production	Price ($)	Production
12337	Camaro Sport Coupe, 6-cyl.	2,466.00	53,523	2,565.00	47,456	2,621.00	34,541
12367	Camaro Convertible, 6-cyl.	2,704.00	5,285	2,802.00	3,513	2,835.00	1,707
12437	Camaro Sport Coupe, 8-cyl.	2,572.00	142,242	2,670.00	167,251	2,727.00	190,971
12467	Camaro Convertible, 8-cyl.	2,809.00	19,856	2,908.00	16,927	2,940.00	15,866
AK1	Custom Deluxe seat and shoulder belts (coupe)	—	—	11.10	22,988	—	—
AL4	Strato-back front bench seat (coupe)	26.35	6,583	32.65	4,896	—	—
AS1	Standard front shoulder belts	23.20	477	23.20	70	23.20	47
AS2	Strato-Ease front seat headrests	52.70	2,342	52.70	2,234	—	—
AS4	Custom Deluxe rear shoulder belts	—	—	26.35	109	26.35	37
AS5	Standard rear shoulder belts	—	—	23.20	24	23.20	78
A01	Soft Ray tinted glass, all windows	30.55	34,725	30.55	65,329	32.65	114,733
A02	Soft Ray tinted windshield glass	21.10	81,998	21.10	60,677	—	—
A31	Power windows	100.10	4,957	100.10	3,304	105.35	3,058
A39	Custom Deluxe front and rear seat belts	6.35	51,247	7.90	3,560	9.00	4,901
A67	Folding rear seat	31.60	17,993	—	—	42.15	4,397
A85	Custom Deluxe front shoulder belts	26.35	894	26.35	222	26.35	922
B37	Color-keyed front and rear floor mats	10.55	23,747	10.55	30,713	11.60	37,158
B93	Door edge guards	3.20	37,964	4.25	49,395	4.25	27,128
CE1	Headlight washer system	—	—	—	—	15.80	116
C06	Power convertible top	52.70	11,783	52.70	9,580	52.70	9,631
C08	Vinyl roof cover (coupe)	73.75	52,455	73.50	77,065	84.30	100,602
C48	Heater and defroster delete	-31.65	2,201				
C50*	Rear window defroster (coupe)	21.10	7,031	21.10	6,181	22.15	7,912
	Rear window defroster (convertible)	—		31.60		32.65	
C60	Air conditioning	356.00	28,226	360.20	35,866	376.00	44,737
C80	Positraction limited-slip differential	42.15	31,792	42.15	36,710	—	—
C94	3.31:1 axle ratio	2.15	1,177	—	—	—	—
C96	3.55:1 axle ratio	2.15	6,322	—	—	—	—
C97	2.73:1 axle ratio	2.15	539	—	—	—	—
DX1	Front accent striping	—	—	—	—	25.30	20,479
D33	Driver's remote-controlled outside mirror	9.50	8,630	9.50	4,740	10.55	7,771
D34	Visor vanity mirror	—	—	—	—	3.20	9,002
D55	Floor-mounted console	47.40	129,477	50.60	140,530	53.75	156,225
D80	Front and rear spoiler equipment	—	—	32.65	15,520	32.65	19,040
D90	Sport striping	—	—	25.30	30,541	25.30	26,729
D91	Front accent band	14.75	24,370	14.75	40,487	—	—
D96	Fender striping	—	—	13.70	19,657	15.80	5,176
F41	Special purpose f&r suspension	10.55	5,968	10.55	7,117	10.55	5,929
G31	HD rear springs	—	—	20.05	821	20.05	556
G80	Positraction limited-slip differential	(See C80)		(See C80)	42.15	48,755	
H01	3.07:1 axle ratio	2.15	560	—	—	—	—
H05	3.73:1 axle ratio	2.15	2,281	—	—	—	—
JL8	Power front and rear disc brakes	—	—	—	—	500.30	206
J50	Power front and rear drum brakes	42.15	24,549	42.15	44,196	42.15	82,890
J52	Power front disc/rear drum brakes	79.00	14,899	100.10	20,117	64.25	67,231
J56	HD front disc/rear metallic drum brakes	105.35	205	—	—	—	—
J65	Front and rear metallic drum brakes	36.90	1,217	—	—	—	—
KD5	HD engine closed positive ventilation system	—	—	6.35	30	6.35	52
K02	Temperature-controlled fan (V-8)	15.80	2,375	15.80	1,285	15.80	1,052
K05	Engine block heater	—	—	—	—	10.55	2,124
K19	Air Injection Reactor (req'd. in CA)	44.75	34,096	—	—	—	—
K24	Engine closed positive ventilation system	5.25	34,503	—	—	—	—
K30	Speed and cruise control	50.05	305	52.70	327	—	—
K76	61-amp Delcotron generator	21.10	136	26.35	90	—	—
K79	42-amp Delcotron generator	10.55	362	10.55	189	10.55	224
K85	63-amp Delcotron generator	—	—	—	—	26.35	114
LM1	350-ci/225-hp Turbo-Fire V-8 engine	—	—	—	—	52.70	10,406
L22	250-ci/155-hp Turbo-Thrift 6-cyl. engine	26.35	38,165	26.35	28,647	26.35	18,660
L30	327-ci/275-hp Turbo-Fire V-8 engine	92.70	25,287	92.70	21,686	—	—
L34	Super SS equip. w/396-ci/350-hp V-8	—	—	368.65	2,579	184.35	2,018
L35	Super SS equip. w/396-ci/325-hp V-8	263.30	4,003	263.30	10,773	63.20	6,752
L48	Super SS equip. w/350-ci/295-hp V-8	210.65	29,270	210.65	12,496	—	22,339
L65	350-ci/250-hp Turbo-Fire V-8 engine	—	—	—	—	21.10	26,898
L78	Super SS equip. w/396-ci/375-hp V-8	500.30	1,138	500.30	4,575	316.00	4,889
L89	Super SS equip. w/L78 396 w/alum. heads	—	—	868.95	272	710.95	311
MB1	Torque-drive transmission (6-cyl.)	—	—	68.65	3,099	68.65	2,186
MC1	Special 3-speed transmission	—	—	—	—	79.00	3,079

RPO/COPO	Description	1967 Model Year Price ($)	1967 Model Year Production	1968 Model Year Price ($)	1968 Model Year Production	1969 Model Year Price ($)	1969 Model Year Production
M11	Floor-mounted shift lever	10.55	12,051	10.55	30,192	10.55	25,586
M13	Special 3-speed manual transmission	79.00	681	79.00	752	—	—
M20	Muncie 4-speed manual trans., wide-ratio	184.35	45,806	184.35	35,161	195.40	37,816
M21	Muncie 4-speed manual trans., close-ratio	184.35	1,733	184.35	11,134	195.40	26,501
M22	HD Muncie 4-speed manual trans., close-ratio	—	—	310.70	1,277	322.10	2,117
M35	PowerGlide automatic transmission	184.35	122,727	184.35	127,165	163.70	78,849
M40	Turbo Hydra-matic automatic transmission	226.45	1,453	237.00	5,466	190.10	66,423
NC8	Chambered dual-exhaust system	—	—	—	—	15.80	1,526
NF2	Dual-exhaust system w/deep-tone mufflers	(See N61)		27.40	9,024	—	—
N10	Dual-exhuast system	21.10	6,722	27.40	4,462	30.55	5,545
N30	Deluxe steering wheel	7.40	30,967	4.25	9,178	—	—
N33	Tilt steering column	42.15	7,980	42.15	5,294	45.30	6,575
N34	Walnut-grained, plastic-rim steering wheel	31.60	8,065	31.60	5,649	34.80	6,883
N40	Power steering	84.30	92,181	84.30	115,280	94.80	141,607
N44	Special quick-ratio steering	15.80	6,155	15.80	3,090	15.80	2,161
N61	Dual-exhaust system w/deep-tone mufflers	21.10	13,748	—	—	—	—
N65	Space Saver spare tire	—	—	19.35	1,021	19.00	2,228
N95	Simulated wire wheel covers	(See P02)		73.75	3,988	73.75	2,118
N96	Mag-style wheel covers	73.75	6,630	73.75	6,072	73.75	2,866
PA2	Mag-spoke–style wheel covers	—	—	73.75	4,085	73.75	1,362
PK8	E78x14 whitewall tires	—	—	—	—	32.10	102,328
PL5	F70x14 white-letter tires	—	—	—	—	63.05	30,605
PQ2	7.35x14 white-stripe tires	52.00	10,913	—	—	—	—
PW6	D70x14 red-stripe tires	62.50	8,330	—	—	—	—
PW7	F70x14 white-stripe tires	—	—	64.75	26,670	62.60	14,457
PW8	F70x14 red-stripe tires	—	—	64.75	6,686	62.60	6,243
PY4	F70x14 fiberglass belted white-stripe tires	—	—	26.55	—	88.60	5,783
PY5	F70x14 fiberglass belted red-stripe tires	—	—	26.55	—	88.60	1,085
P01	Bright metal wheel covers	21.10	137,163	21.10	133,742	21.10	106,386
P02	Simulated wire wheel covers	73.75	6,577	—	—	—	—
P06	Wheel trim rings	—	—	—	—	21.10	2,401
P12	14x6 Rally Wheels (5)	5.30	3,667	—	—	—	—
P58	7.35x14 whitewall tires	31.35	138,998	31.35	141,178	—	—
T60	Heavy-duty battery	7.40	7,964	7.40	8,196	8.45	9,738
U03	3-volume horn (coupe)	13.70	1,580	13.70	768	—	—
U15	Speed warning indicator	10.55	3,698	10.55	2,344	11.60	2,111
U16	Tachometer	—	—	—	—	52.70	1,410
U17	Console-mounted instrument cluster (V-8)	79.00	27,078	94.80	20,263	94.80	29,524
U25	Trunk light	2.65	24,787	—	—	—	—
U26	Engine compartment light	2.65	22,965	—	—	—	—
U27	Glovebox light	2.65	11,032	—	—	—	—
U28	Ashtray light	1.65	25,538	—	—	—	—
U29	Courtesy lights (coupe)	4.25	23,691	—	—	—	—
U35	Electric clock	15.80	13,185	15.80	20,319	15.80	20,330
U46	Light monitoring system	—	—	26.35	1,755	26.35	1,450
U57	Stereo tape system	128.50	2,746	133.80	4,155	133.80	6,239
U63	AM push-button radio	57.40	174,021	61.10	192,805	61.10	206,598
U69	AM-FM push-button radio	133.80	6,232	133.80	7,214	133.80	8,271
U73	Rear-mount antenna	9.50	32,223	9.50	21,729	9.50	16,394
U79	AM-FM stereo radio	—	—	239.15	1,335	239.10	2,359
U80	Rear seat speaker	13.20	27,701	13.20	23,198	13.20	26,862
VE3	Body-color Endura front bumper	—	—	—	—	42.15	12,650
V01	Heavy-duty radiator	10.55	6,190	13.70	4,682	14.75	3,802
V31	Front bumper guards	12.65	35,154	12.65	19,455	12.65	12,657
V32	Rear bumper guards	9.50	35,029	12.65	18,628	12.65	12,369
V75	Liquid tire chain	—	—	—	—	23.20	188
ZJ7	Rally wheels	—	—	31.60	8,047	35.85	48,735
ZJ9	Auxiliary lighting group	—	—	13.70	18,099	13.70	15,768
ZK3	Custom Deluxe seat and shoulder belts (coupe)	—	—	—	—	12.15	18,760
ZL2	Super Scoop special ducted hood	—	—	—	—	79.00	10,026
Z10	Indy Sport Coupe accents	—	—	—	—	36.90	na
Z11	Indy Sport Convertible accents	—	—	—	—	36.90	3,675
Z21	Style trim group	40.05	79,016	42.15	93,235	47.40	102,740
Z22	Rally Sport package	105.35	64,842	105.35	40,977	131.65	37,773
Z23	Interior style trim group	10.55	74,648	57,098.00	18	17.95	66,469
Z27	Super Sport Equipment	—	—	—	—	295.95	34,932
Z28	Special Performance package (coupe)	358.10	602	400.25	7,199	458.15	20,302
Z87	Custom Deluxe interior	94.80	69,103	110.60	50,461	110.60	39,875
	Two-tone paint	—	—	—	—	31.60	5,909
9560	Special Performance V-8 (ZL1 427-ci/425-hp)	—	—	—	—	4,160.15	69
9561†	Special Performance V-8 (L72 427-ci/425-hp)	—	—	na	na	489.75	1,015
9737	Sports Car Conversion	—	—	na	na	184.70	na

*Coupe production figure includes convertible production, as well. † Includes 201 Yenko Super Camaros built under COPOs 9561 & 9737

APPENDIX D
DECODING 1967–1969 PROTECT-O-PLATE WARRANTY PLATES

1967 CAMARO PROTECT-O-PLATE WARRANTY PLATE CODES

Location	Data	Code(s)	Description/Note(s)
A	Interior Color*	A	Red vinyl
		B	Blue
		C	Black vinyl
		D	Red
		E	Black
		F*	Fawn
		G	Gold
		H	Blue vinyl
		K	Parchment/Black
		L	Black vinyl
		M*	Maroon
		N	Black cloth
		P*	Plum
		R	Bright Blue
		S*	Blue cloth
		T	Turquoise
		U	Blue vinyl (optional)
		V*	Fawn vinyl
		W*	Gold cloth
		Y	Yellow
B/C	Lower/Upper Body Colors	A	Tuxedo Black
		C	Ermine White
		D	Nantucket Blue
		E	Deepwater Blue
		F	Marina Blue
		G	Granada Gold
		H	Mountain Green
		K	Emerald Turquoise
		L	Tahoe Turquoise
		M	Royal Plum
		N	Madiera Maroon
		R	Bolero Red
		S	Sierra Fawn
		T	Capri Cream
		Y	Butternut Yellow
D	VIN	Must match Vehicle Identification Number	
E	Carburetor Source	C	Carter
		H	Holley
		R	Rochester
F	Engine Number	Matches stamping on engine ID pad	
G	Rear Axle	Matches stamping on axle tube	
H	Build Month	K	November, 1966
		L	September, 1966
		N	April, 1967
		P	February, 1967
		R	October, 1966
		S	January, 1967
		T	June, 1967
		V	August, 1966
		W	March, 1967
		X	July, 1967
		Y	May, 1967
		Z	December, 1966

Location	Data	Code(s)	Description/Note(s)
I	Transmission #	Matches stamping on transmission ID pad	
J	Power Accessories	1	Power Steering (N40) only
		2	Power Brakes (J50) only
		3	Power Brakes & Power Steering
K	Radio/Clock Group	1	Camaro, Chevelle, Chevrolet, Chevy II, Corvair
L	Radio	3	AM Radio (U63)
		4	U63 w/rear speaker (U80)
		5	AM/FM Radio (U69)
		6	U69 w/rear speaker (U80)
M	Disc Brakes	3	Disc brakes (J52)
		5	Spec. Suspension (F41) w/J52
N	Air Conditioning	1	Air Conditioning (C60)
		4	Heater delete (C48)
O	Power Windows	1	Power Windows (A31)
		5	Door Edge Guards w/A31
P	Power Seats	Not available on Camaro	
Q	Bowtie Logo		

*Limitied availability discontinued during production run as stock was exhausted

1967-1969 Protect-O-Plates

DⒶⒷCCCⒸ   124377N102345   Ⓓ   HⒺ

T0414MQⒻ   PJ0323GⒼ   NⒽ

P7C20Ⓘ   2ⓈⓀⓁⓂⓃⓄⓅ1554   Ⓠ

JOHN A DOE
123 ELM ST #2
SPRINGFLD MASS 2-21-67
USA

1968 Camaro Protect-O-Plate Warranty Plate Codes

Location	Data	Code(s)	Description/Note(s)
A	Interior Color	B	Blue (cloth or vinyl)
		D	Red (cloth or vinyl)
		E	Black (cloth or vinyl)
		G	Gold (cloth or vinyl)
		K	Parchment/Black
		P	Gold vinyl (optional)
		Q	Black/White vinyl (optional)
		T	Turquoise (cloth or vinyl)
		U	Blue vinyl (optional)
B/C	Lower/Upper Body Colors	A	Tuxedo Black
		C	Ermine White
		D	Grotto Blue
		E	Fathom Blue
		F	Island Teal
		G	Ash Gold
		H	Grecian Green
		J	Rallye Green
		K	Tripoli Turquoise
		L	Teal Blue
		N	Cordovan Maroon
		O	Corvette Bronze
		P	Seafrost Green
		R	Matador Red
		T	Palomino Ivory
		U	LeMans Blue
		V	Sequoia Green
		Y	Butternut Yellow
		Z	British Green
		(blank) or - -	Special Order Paint
D	VIN		Must match Vehicle Identification Number
E	Carburetor Source	C	Carter
		H	Holley
		R	Rochester

Location	Data	Code(s)	Description/Note(s)
F	Engine Number		Matches stamping on engine ID pad
G	Rear Axle		Matches stamping on axle tube
H	Build Month	1	January, 1968
		2	February, 1968
		3	March, 1968
		4	April, 1968
		5	May, 1968
		6	June, 1968
		7	July, 1968
		8	August, 1967
		9	September, 1967
		0	October, 1967
		N	November, 1967
		D	December, 1967
I	Transmission #		Matches stamping on transmission ID pad
J	Power Accessories	1	Power Steering (N40) only
		2	Power Brakes (J50) only
		3	Power Brakes & Power Steering
K	Unused	(blank)	
L	Radio	4	AM Radio (U63) w/r. spkr. (U80)
		5	AM/FM Radio (U69)
		6	U69 w/U80
		7	U69 w/stereo (U79)
M	Disc Brakes	3	Disc brakes (J52)
		5	Spec. Suspension (F41) w/J52
		6	Heavy-Duty Disc Brakes (J56)
		7	F41 w/J56
		9	J52 w/metallic rear shoes (J56)
N	Air Conditioning	1	Air Conditioning (C60)
		4	Heater delete (C48)
O	Accessories	1	Power Windows (A31)
		5	Space Saver Spare (N65) w/A31
P	Power Seats		Not available on Camaro
Q	Bowtie Logo		

1969 Camaro Protect-O-Plate Warranty Plate Codes

Location	Data	Code(s)	Description/Note(s)
A	Not Used		
B	Not Used		
C	Not Used		
D	VIN		Must match Vehicle Identification Number
E	Carburetor Source	C	Carter
		H	Holley
		R	Rochester
F	Engine Number		Matches stamping on engine ID pad
G	Rear Axle		Matches stamping on axle tube
H	Assembly Month	1	January, 1969
		2	February, 1969
		3	March, 1969
		4	April, 1969
		5	May, 1969
		6	June, 1969
		7	July, 1969
		8	August, 1968 or 1969
		9	September, 1968 or 1969
		0	October, 1968 or 1969
		N	November, 1968 or 1969
		D	December, 1968 or 1969
I	Transmission #		Matches stamping on transmission ID pad
J	Power Steering	1	Power Steering (N40)
K	Power Brakes	1	Power Brakes (J50)
L	Radio	3	AM Radio (U63), or AM/FM Radio (U69), or AM/FM Stereo (U79)
M	Disc Brakes	3	Disc Brakes, Front (J52)
N	Air Conditioning	1	Air Conditioning (C60)
O	Power Windows	3	Air Conditioning (C60)
P	Power Seats		Not available on Camaro
Q	Bowtie Logo		

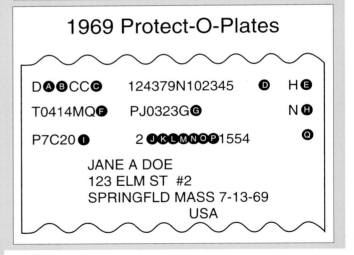

Appendix E
1967–1969 Chevrolet Camaro Coupe
General Specifications and Dimensions

	1967	1968	1969
Overall Length (in.)	184.7	184.6	186.0
Overall Width (in.)	72.5	72.3	74.0
Overall Height (in.)	51.4	50.9	51.6
Wheelbase (in.)	108.0	108.0	108.0
Front Tread (in.)	59.0	59.6	59.6
Rear Tread (in.)	58.9	59.5	59.5
Curb Weight (lbs.)	2,910.0	2,950.0	3,120.0
Trunk Cargo Area (cu. ft.)	8.3	8.3	8.5
Fuel Capacity (gal.)	18.0	18.0	18.0

APPENDIX F
1967–1969 CAMARO ENGINE CODES

(stamped into machined pad on cylinder case at time of engine manufacture)

Year(s)	Displacement	Horsepower	Torque	Carburetion	Powertrain Configuration	Code	RPO*
1967	283**	195		1-2 bbl.	4-spd.	MD	
					Powerglide	MJ	
	302	290	290	1-4 bbl.	SHP; 4-spd.	MO	Z28
					SHP; 4-spd.; AIR	MP	
	327	210		1-2 bbl.	3-, 4-spd.	MA	
					3-, 4-spd.; AIR	MB	
					Powerglide	ME	
					Powerglide; AIR	MF	
		275		1-4 bbl.	3-, 4-spd.	MK	
					3-, 4-spd.; AIR	ML	
					Powerglide	MM	
					Powerglide; AIR	MN	
	350	295		1-4 bbl.	3-, 4-spd.	MS	
					3-, 4-spd.; AIR	MT	
					Powerglide	MU	
					Powerglide; AIR	MV	
	396	325		1-4 bbl.	HD 3-spd., HD 4-spd.	MW	
					HD 3-spd., HD 4-spd.; AIR	MX	
					Turbohydramatic	MY	
					Turbohydramatic	MZ	
		375		1-4 bbl.	SHP; 4-spd.	MQ	L78
					SHP; 4-spd. w/AIR	MR	
1968	302	290	290	1-4 bbl.	SHP; 4-spd., AIR	MO	Z28
	327	210		1-2 bbl.	3-, 4-spd.	MA	
					Powerglide	ME	
		275		1-4 bbl.	3-, 4-spd.	EA	
					Powerglide	EE	
	350	295		1-4 bbl.	3-, 4-spd.	MS	
					Powerglide	MU	
	396	325		1-4 bbl.	3-, 4-spd.	MW	
					Turbohydramatic	MY	
		350		1-4 bbl.	3-, 4-spd.	MX	
					HP; Turbohydramatic	MR	
		375		1-4 bbl.	SHP	MQ	L79
					SHP; alum. cyl. heads		L89
	427	425		1-4 bbl.	4-spd.		9561†
					Turbohydramatic		
1969	302	290	290	1-4 bbl.	SHP; 4-spd.; AIR	DZ	Z28
	307	200		1-2 bbl.	3-, 4-spd.	DA	
					Powerglide	DC	
					Turbohydramatic 350	DD	
					4-spd.	DE	
	327	210		1-2 bbl.	3-, 4-spd.	FJ	
					Powerglide	FK	
					Turbohydramatic 350	FL	
					Low-compression engine; 3-spd.	FS	
					Low-compression engine; Powerglide	FT	
	350	250		1-2 bbl.	3-, 4-spd.	HC	
					Turbohydramatic 350	HD	
					Powerglide	HF	
		255		1-2 bbl.	3-, 4-spd.	HQ	
					Powerglide	HR	
					Turbohydramatic 350	HS	
		300		1-4 bbl.	HP; 3-, 4-spd.	HA	
					HP; Turbohydramatic 350	HB	
					HP; Powerglide	HE	
					HP; HD clutch	HP	
	396	325		1-4 bbl.	3-, 4-spd.	JB	
					Turbohydramatic 400	JG	
					3-, 4-spd.; HD clutch	JU	
		350		1-4 bbl.	HP; 3-, 4-spd.	JF	
					HP; Turbohydramatic 400	JI	
					HP; 3-, 4-spd.; HD clutch	KA	
		375		1-4 bbl.	SHP; 3-, 4-spd.	JH	L78
					SHP; alum. cyl. heads; 4-spd.	JJ	L89
					SHP; Turbohydramatic 400	JL	L78
					SHP; alum. cyl. heads; TH 400	JM	L89
					SHP; 3-, 4-spd.; HD clutch	KC	
					SHP; alum. cyl. heads; HD clutch	KE	
	427	425		1-4 bbl.	SHP; 4-spd.	MN	9561†
					SHP; Turbohydramatic 400	MO	
		430		1-4 bbl.	SHP; 4-spd.	ML	9560†
					SHP; Turbohydramatic 400	MM	

*Some engines were included as part of an option package; in those cases the package's RPO code is given. **Tonawanda plant records indicate a total of 193 283 engines were built for Camaro production: 72 code MD and 121 code MJ. † Available by Central Office Production Order (COPO) only.

Index